MIDWINTER
FOLK
TALES

T0352636

MIDWINTER
FOLK
TALES

TAFFY THOMAS

The
History
Press

First published 2014

Reprinted 2019

The History Press
The Mill, Brimscombe Port
Stroud, Gloucestershire, GL5 2QG
www.thehistorypress.co.uk

British Library Cataloguing in Publication Data.
A catalogue record for this book is available from the British Library.

ISBN 978 0 7509 5588 1

Typesetting and origination by The History Press
Printed in Great Britain by TJ International Ltd, Padstow, Cornwall.

This collection of folk tales is dedicated to all who love to tell stories by a fire in the heart of winter, and, of course, those who love to listen to them or read them by that same fire.

For,

'Winter is the time for comfort, for good food and warmth, for the touch of a friendly hand and a talk beside the fire, it is the time for home.'

Edith Sitwell

CONTENTS

PROLOGUE

Winter

A wrinkled, crabbed man they picture thee,
Old Winter, with a rugged beard as grey
As long moss upon the apple tree;
Blue lipt, an ice-drop at thy sharp blue nose;
Close muffled up, and on the dreary way,
Plodding alone through sleet and drifting snows.

They should have drawn thee by the high-heapt hearth,
Old Winter! Seated in thy great armed chair,
Watching the children at their Christmas mirth,
Or circled by them, as thy lips declare
Some merry jest, or tale of murder dire,
Or troubled spirit that disturbs the night,
Pausing at times to rouse the mouldering fire,
Or taste the old October brown and bright.

Robert Southey (1774–1843) wrote those stanzas in Cumbria as Poet Laureate and friend of the Romantics such as Wordsworth and Coleridge. In his book Bygone Cumberland and Westmorland *(1899) a lesser-known writer, Daniel Scott, wrote:*

Christmas at Lakeland

The labouring ox is said to kneel at twelve o'clock at night, preceding the day of the nativity: the bees are heard to sing at the same hour. On the morn of Christmas Day breakfast early on hack-pudding, a mess made of sheep's heart mixed with suet and sweet fruits.

FOREWORD

Taffy Thomas is a never-ending giver, a beloved communicator of the highest order and – because of his stories but most particularly because of him – we all live happily ever after.

I hope the words of my winter song that follows create the perfect climate for this collection of Taffy's *Midwinter Folk Tales*.

The Snow Falls

Cruel winter cuts through like a reaper,
The old year lies withered and slain,
Like Barleycorn who rose from the grave
The New Year will rise up again.

And the snow falls
And the wind calls
And the year turns round again.

And I'll wager a hatful of guineas
Against all of the songs you can sing
Someday you'll love
And the next day you'll lose
And Winter will turn into Spring.

And the snow falls
And the wind calls
And the year turns round again.

There will come a time of great plenty
A time of good harvest and song
Til then put your trust in tomorrow, my friend,
For Yesterday's over and done.

And the snow falls
And the wind calls
And the year turns round again.

John Tams

PREFACE

When I am considering the extent to which the television has damaged our rich oral tradition of storytelling, I often think that while there is truth in this, perhaps the reduction in the numbers of open fires in private living rooms, bars, cafes and restaurants has done just as much, if not more damage. Wherever there is a fire, folk cluster round it and yarn. Wherever folk yarn they resort to storytelling, because most treasured knowledge of families and communities survives by being encapsulated in a narrative tale.

Right from childhood, both my parents' and my grandparents' houses were sometimes chilly. The open fire, therefore, was the heart of the house: that and the dining table. I learned to embrace the fact that the British climate – then bitter in winter and warmer in spring and summer – provided a rich seasonal variety. I actually enjoyed wearing thick woolly jumpers and corduroy trousers in winter, and relished the opportunity to read or talk by the fire. When spring and summer came, the switch to short trousers and cotton short-sleeved shirts to toss a ball around outdoors for all the hours of daylight was something to celebrate. I was horrified when my godfather, Uncle Jack, an RAF boffin, converted his house so that it would be the same comfortable temperature every day of the year. How comfortable, but how boring!

If you embrace seasonal variety, this will be reflected in the stories you choose to tell or hear at any point in the year. This is my winter collection.

Whenever two Englishmen meet, they discuss the weather; I love this. A northern friend of mine often glances sideways at the sky whilst muttering, 'It looks a bit rough over Bill's mother's'. There is also the old adage that if you can see the mountain tops it's going to rain, while if you can't see them, it's already raining. With such cultural riches, Part 1 comprises tales linked to the often-inclement weather. Part 2 is bursting at the seams with magic and contains most of my extensive Christmas repertoire, which only surfaces annually from Advent to Twelfth Night, unlike the shops who 'do' Christmas from Halloween to Easter. The Nativity legends have been gleaned from ancient carols, and when told have provided ground bait for relative strangers to gift me gems like 'The Christmas Cat' and 'The Legend of Tinsel'. For me, every year Christmas starts when I tell 'The Legend of the Robin' and 'The Legend of Tinsel'.

As the fireside is a place for fun and games as well as stories during a time when families are together, Part 3, which includes riddles and riddle stories, will get you thinking at a time when most people's riddles come from Christmas crackers.

If people are gathered by a fire, a ghost story is often the outcome. Probably thanks to Charles Dickens, there is a link between Christmas and ghost stories; hence Part 4.

There is something about New Year that heralds the opportunity for a fresh start, and the stories in Part 5 reflect a desire for a better and more peaceful future. They also acknowledge the fact that the change from the Julian to the Gregorian calendar in 1752 has left us with 17 January as 'Old Twelfth Night'. Consequently, in the West Country (my birthplace), wassailing and some Yule log customs, all of which are a voice for a happier and healthier new year, take place in January.

'Warm Words on a Cold Night', a toast I discovered on the wall of the Guinness brewery in Dublin, is something I wish for all of my readers – that and the inspiration to retell the stories, for if they were all presents to me, they are also presents from me.

Taffy Thomas,
9 January 2014

ACKNOWLEDGEMENTS

As a touring storyteller in the oral tradition, I am only able to deliver my 250 or so performances a year with support. This is made even more necessary by the fact that my personal odyssey included a massive stroke at the age of 36. I am supported in my journeys and shows by my wife Chrissy who generously gave up her own life running a dance studio to help me reinvent myself from the time I couldn't walk, couldn't talk, and couldn't use a knife and fork. I have a number of storytelling mentors, including the wildly eccentric Ruth Tongue, who I met in Somerset when I was but a lad. Later in my storytelling journey, two of Scotland's Travelling People, Betsy Whyte and Duncan Williamson, became both sources of stories and massive influences. As my award-winning 'Ancestral Voices' performance begins …

> 'If I stand tall, it is because I am standing on the
> shoulders of those that have gone before.'

Many of my other major influences are credited in the introductions to tales they have generously passed in my direction.

As a writer I have again a number of influences and mentors. Firstly my wife Chrissy is my muse, occasional censor and tireless support. She has also taught herself to utilise if not love the computer – a tool I have so far chosen to ignore. All the stories in this section started off being told before they became painstak-ingly handwritten versions in my ever-mounting pile of exercise books – sorry trees! In an attempt to keep a storyteller's voice, in developing the next stage from exercise book to computer, I half dictate and half tell each tale to one of my volunteer electro-scribes. Chrissy again heads this team, along with our youngest daughter Rosie and our part-time PA Tony Farren. The bulk of the time on the keyboard, however, has fallen upon our friend and volunteer helper Sue Leeming. The next stage is when the copy is e-mailed to the generous and ridiculously talented Steven Gregg who almost instantly e-mails back a magical illustration before shaping the ever-growing file of tales and illustrations into a manuscript. Without him this book would probably have never reached com-pletion. My mentor in writing and publishing is the wonderful Helen Watts of Aston Hill Editorial, near Stratford-on-Avon. She is a helpful, positive critic and an inspiration to me through her own writing. Declan Flynn and the team at The History Press are kind enough to publish me, encourage me, and cope with my pestering phone calls in the knowledge that I don't really do e-mails. As a storyteller, I prefer talking to people.

Two inspiring songwriters, John Tams and Dave Goulder, were kind enough to allow me to quote two of their finest pieces of work to top and tail this collection. Their reward will be on licensed premises when next we meet! As a storyteller passionate about the oral tradition, I will continue to tell and write folk tales – presenting and preserving that tradition for as long as I am able. Knowing this, perhaps the bulk of my gratitude should go to you my listeners and readers. If you like the stories then have a go at passing them on and take your place in a truly spellbinding chain.

ILLUSTRATIONS

The illustrations have been drawn by young Cumbrian artist Steven Gregg.

> Winter is one of my favourite times of the year, when the nights roll in and I dig out my warm clothing and wrap up tight. It's a season where the world surrounds us with such rich imagery; leafless trees, frost creeping up the windows, birds all puffed up to contend with the chill.
>
> With this, I jumped at the chance to collaborate with Taffy and The History Press again on another folk tales book. Casting my pen across a mighty dragon, all the way down to the tiniest spider. What more proof do you need to see that Winter inspires creativity?
>
> *Steven Gregg*

The cover illustration has been created by Katherine Soutar, who has done the covers for the whole collection of the folk tales series.

The image for the wassailing recipe was produced by John Crane, who has had a long association with the storytelling centre, providing images for so many of its publications.

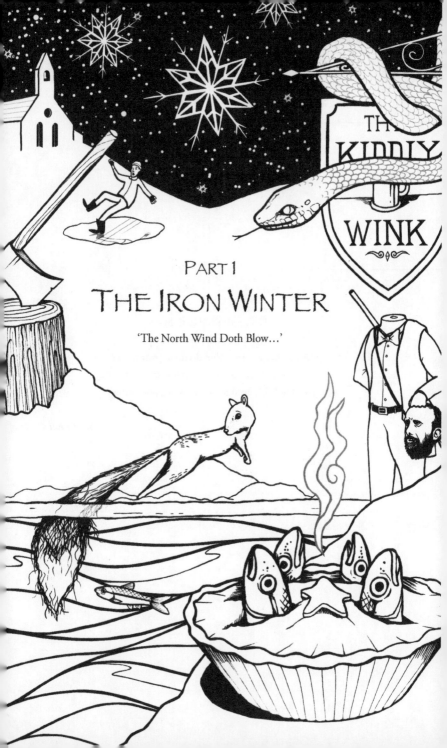

PART 1
THE IRON WINTER

'The North Wind Doth Blow...'

The north wind doth blow,
And we shall have snow,
And what will the robin do then, poor thing?
He'll sit in the barn to keep himself warm,
And hide his head under his wing, poor thing.

Traditional

St Nicholas

St Nicholas was a bishop of the early Church. There are many legends of this picturesque character with his long white beard and bright eyes. Several of these legends include the hanging up of stockings to be filled with presents. St Nicholas Day falls on 6 December, a day when many European children receive their gifts.

The story that follows, however, was gifted to me on a visit to my Shropshire storytelling friends. If it was a present to me, then it is a present from me. Please take this story as a gift and tell it.

Many years ago there was a hotel in Russia famous for its food and hospitality. The hotel owner was rich and popular.

It was the iron winter and the snow was so deep you could lean on it. Every room in the hotel was prepared for a guest and there was a big pot of soup bubbling on the hob, but no travellers could get there. The hotel owner was rattling around the big building alone. As the clock ticked towards midnight, there was a knocking on the heavy oak door. As the hotelier opened the door, he discovered a tramp – an old man with bright blue eyes, a long white beard and a ragged red coat. The tramp begged for a bite to eat and a bed for the night. The hotel owner told him he could 'just about squeeze him in', but it would cost him three roubles. The tramp turned out his pockets, finding them empty. He told the hotel owner he had no money but promised he would pay the debt as soon as he could. If he wasn't helped, he would surely perish in the snow.

The hotel owner took pity on the tramp, leading him into the warm hotel and sitting him on a big wooden chair by the fire. He brought the hungry old man a big steaming bowl of borscht – beetroot soup with a twist of sour cream – and half a loaf of rye bread. The tramp devoured the soup greedily. It was the first food he'd had for more than a week. In fact, he ate it so voraciously that the beetroot left a red stain on his white moustache. He wiped his mouth with the back of his hand, thanking the hotelier for his kindness and again repeating his promise to pay him as soon as he could. He would be leaving with the first light of day.

After a good night's sleep in a comfortable bed, the tramp was up and away with the first light of day. Seeing the footprints in the snow disappearing up the road, the hotelier thought he would never see the three roubles he was owed.

Strangely, that very day the snow melted and folk could again travel to the hotel. Trade picked up and the hotel owner wanted to go to the cathedral to say a prayer of thanks for his new-found luck. He walked the twenty miles to Moscow City, to the great cathedral. As he walked through the gate in the city walls, the cathedral bells rang. Up the stone steps the hotelier went and opened the great wooden doors of the church. The walls of the cathedral were covered with icons, beautiful paintings of the saints, decorated with real gold leaf. One picture diagonally across the nave drew the hotelier towards it. It was a picture of an old man with a long white beard, bright blue eyes and a ragged red coat, a man strangely familiar to him. It was indeed the image of the old tramp the hotelier had helped the previous night. The hotel owner decided to say his prayer of thanks in front of that picture. He bought a candle and stooped to press the candle in the shallow sand tray in front of the picture. The candle bumped against something. Flicking the sand away with his fingers, he discovered three rouble coins. The old tramp had kept his promise. Pocketing the coins, the hotelier completed his prayer and looked at the painting for one last time. At the base of the picture there were two words written, the name of the old man. Those two words read 'St Nicholas'.

In Russia he is called St Nicholas, in France he is called Papa Noel, in Germany he is called Sinter Claus, in America that becomes Santa Claus but we just call him Father Christmas.

Jack Turnip

The following story concerns Jack Turnip, an anti-hero whose vain pride leads to a 'fall' on the ice. I first heard it from one of the Company of Storytellers, a trio of 'Performance Storytellers' who have specialised in taking oral storytelling to a primarily adult audience. That said, I have discovered that children love this tale. Why wouldn't they when the protagonist falls on his bottom?

It was the iron winter. Jack Turnip sat in the grandfather chair in his tiny cottage and shivered. The hearth was lifeless and the log basket empty. His heavy axe stood patiently in the corner of the room. Jack knew what he had to do. He also knew that logs warm you three times: firstly they warm you when you wield the axe, then they further warm you when you lug them home; only then do they truly warm you as you sit by the fire.

Donning his hat and scarf, Jack set off confidently up the lane. In a daydream, and thinking of how much work he might achieve in a day, Jack didn't notice the frozen puddle on the path. He keeled over on the ice, landing flat on his backside! Collecting his scrambled senses he cursed the ice, regretting it was stronger than him – *or so it would seem*. Then he pondered that although it was midwinter, the sun would soon rise in the sky and gain the strength to melt the ice. Therefore the sun was the strongest – *or so it would seem*. Jack, something of a bar room philosopher, continued his train of thought. He pondered that even in spring clouds could block out the sun, so clouds must be the strongest – *or so it would seem*. He reasoned March winds might be strong and they could chase the clouds, so the winds were the strongest – *or so it would seem*. Ahead of him, Jack could see the mountain that overshadowed his tiny cottage. He ruminated a little wind couldn't blow away the mountain, so the mountain was the strongest – *or so it would seem*. On top of the peak, silhouetted against the skyline, was a hardy tree. Jack thought that a tree could grow on a mountain, but a mountain couldn't grow on a tree. Therefore the tree was the strongest – *or so it would seem*. Feeling the weight of the axe on his shoulder, Jack walked towards the tree and swung the axe, felling the fir giant in three mighty blows.

Jack stood triumphant with the axe above his head, bragging to the heavens that he was the strongest – *or so it would seem*.

Full of himself, and more than a little hungry and thirsty, Jack headed full tilt down the path that headed towards home. He was so much of a boaster and poser that he didn't notice the frozen puddle on the path. He slid dramatically, landing flat on his bottom.

All he could do was grab a couple of sticks, crawl home and sit by his meagre fire pondering his mishap.

Adam's Fall

This story hails from Cornwall and I first heard it as a narrative song. It was sung at the Sidmouth Folk Festival in the 1960s by Mrs Foxworthy (mother to my friend, folklorist Tony Foxworthy). She was always known as Mrs Foxworthy, even to those who knew her well – old school! She carried on singing it for the full century of her life. I have put it back into a rhossum (the word Ruth Tongue used to denote short humorous stories of local characters) and it may well have started life in this form before a Cornish dialect enthusiast fashioned it into a song. The song is now kept alive by Cornish singer and story-teller Mo Keest of Bodmin, who also got it from Mrs Foxworthy.

Like Jack Turnip in the previous story, the anti-hero comes to grief on the ice.

Adam Trelawny and his wife Morwenna lived in the tiny Cornish village of Blisland. Like most Cornish villages, the devotions of the locals had been much influenced by the Wesley brothers John and Charles. If most of the locals were 'chapel', Morwenna Trelawny was 'church' and much looked forward to a weekly visit to their tiny cottage from the Reverend Tremayne, who would deliver a scripture in exchange for a cup of tea and a saffron bun. If most folk were 'chapel' and his wife was 'church', Adam was 'pub' and disappeared to the Kiddly-wink whenever possible, especially when the winter weather started to bite and he could warm himself with several large glasses of Rum and Shrub.

One December day, after a liquid lunch, Adam was making his way home. Droozled with drink, he didn't spot the large frozen puddle by the oak tree. He slid sideways, cracking his skull bone on the lower branches of the tree. Bruised and bleeding from the rough bark, Adam picked himself up and continued home. Morwenna cussed him before cleaning him up and binding his head with vinegar and brown paper to bring out the bruising.

Wouldn't you know it, no sooner had Morwenna completed her nursing when she spotted the Reverend Tremayne making his way up the path to deliver his scripture and enjoy his saffron bun.

In shame Morwenna hid her battered husband – who still had the aroma of Nelson's Blood (rum – his favourite tipple) about him – under the stairs. She opened the door to the smiling parson and handed him his tea before eagerly requesting the scripture of the day. Reverend Tremayne asked her if she had heard about Adam's fall. Shocked and guilt-ridden, Morwenna told her husband he might as well come out from hiding as the parson had already heard about it all! The battered Adam appeared from under the stairs bruised and humbled. The parson intoned Genesis, Chapter 3 and had just reached '… cursed is the ground for thy sake; in sorrow shalt thou eat of it all the days of thy life.'

Morwenna listened devoutly but Adam just looked confused.

Fish, Flesh or Fowl

The story that follows is the only tale in my extensive repertoire that I tell in the first person. This is because, during my thirty-five years in Cumbria, I have been influenced by the tradition of elaborate lying stories. The 'World's Biggest Liar' competition has been held in Wasdale, Cumbria for thirty years. The bones of the story came to me from John Campbell, sheep farmer and genius purveyor of tales from Mullaghbawn, Northern Ireland. His passing has done nothing to dim the memories of the delight he gave every audience I ever saw him face.

As an experienced storyteller in my sixties, I manage to bash out a simple living for my wife, children and myself by performing several days a week in schools, universities, village halls or wherever an audience fancy an hour or so of simple honest storytelling with few frills. It was not always so easy, however. As Christmas approached one year, the diary had gone through a lean spell and the fridge was empty. In fact, things had got so bad that if my wife wanted to get anything out of the deep freeze, I had to hold on to her ankles! The tension between us built up and to be brutally frank I was given my marching orders and told not to return to our small cottage unless I could bring fish, flesh and fowl. Thirty-eight years old at the time, I was forced to turn hunter-gatherer. As if that wasn't bad enough, it was the iron winter. Standing in the ice in Hollens Yard, I pondered what to do. I reasoned there could well be ducks on Grasmere lake and maybe a rabbit or two in the banking, and perhaps a trout or salmon in the beck: but how to catch them? Seeking spiritual support I thought of the village rector, Dr Bevan, who had been supportive in the past – having been my wife Chrissy's chaplain during her time at Durham University. I remember that over his fireplace in the rectory he kept an antique firearm, a Queen Anne muzzle-loading gun, I suspected that although ancient it was in full working order … the Revd Bev was like that. Perhaps I could borrow it.

Enthused by this thought, maybe there is a bit of hunter-gatherer in every man, I made my way down to the rectory. I knocked thoughtfully on the iron knocker. After a long pause and a creaking of floorboards, the door was opened slowly by the venerable churchman. Of course he enquired after my wife's wellbeing and was saddened to hear of my plight. Keen to help, he invited me indoors. I was delighted to observe that the old gun was still there on the wall. He agreed to lend it to me providing I allowed him to give me a lesson on the correct way to use such an ancient beast. More than a little excited, I agreed. The cleric stood the ancient firearm with the butt by his boot. From the barrel he meaningfully drew a rod and, flicking it under his right armpit, stated 'this is the ramrod!' Turning, he seized an old horn from the mantle shelf and cupping his left hand around the barrel of the gun, funnelled a goodish amount of black powder down the barrel. He then told me I needed some wadding. When I looked mystified, he pulled out his shirt tail and, tearing off a bit of white cotton, stuffed it down the barrel. He whipped the ramrod from under his armpit and produced a number of thrusting movements with it down the barrel. I now realised why it was called a ramrod. He directed me that the ramrod should immediately be removed and replaced under the armpit. From his jingling, copious tweed jacket pocket he took a handful of ball bearings. These rattled down the barrel. More wadding was required, so his other shirt tail was sacrificed. More ramming ensued, then once again the insistence that the ramrod be removed and replaced under the armpit. The weapon was now fully prepared for cocking and firing. As this was just a demonstration, the old chap disabled it and handed me the weapon and all the necessary accoutrements: ramrod, powder horn and a hand full of balls. He again reminded me to remove the ramrod at every stage of the operation. With the gun under one arm, the ramrod under the other and pockets jangling full of ball bearings, I attached the powder horn professionally to my belt. I warmly thanked the Revd Bev for his help and planned the next stage of my offensive against Lakeland's edible game. The lake was the most likely place for me to join the ranks of the like of Buffalo Bill Cody, Wild Bill Hickock or even the famous John Peel. My place in self-sufficiency folklore was secure.

However, it was the iron winter. When I reached the lake, it was frozen solid. Half a dozen confused mallards were trying unsuccessfully to emulate Torvil and Dean right in the middle. I decided they were fowl and they were edible. I needed to move quickly. Drawing on the memory of the Revd Bev's firearm lesson, I stood the gun upright by my boot. With almost military precision I flicked the ramrod under my right armpit. Despite a fierce wind, most of the black powder I tipped from the powder horn went down the barrel. Whipping out my shirt tail caused a sharp draught up my back; with powder and wadding in the gun, it was time for the ramming. The ducks had spotted me by now and were getting fractious. Trying not to panic, I replaced the ramrod under my armpit. A handful of ball bearings rattled down the barrel followed by a bit more wadding and some earnest ramming. By now the ducks were airborne across the lake. In panic I forgot to remove the ramrod and merely pointed the gun and pulled the trigger. The explosion that immediately followed was sufficient to knock me backwards, head over heels on the lake shore. To my surprise I landed on something soft. Looking behind me I realised I had landed on a large jack hare, breaking its neck and killing it stone cold dead. It was flesh. I tucked it in my poacher's shoulder bag before looking across the ice to behold six ducks all falling downwards, skewered by my ramrod. I had got all of them with one shot and a hare as well. The downside was that the mallards fell on to the ice in the middle of the lake. I would have to retrieve them. Walking gingerly over the ice, I was unsettled by a cracking sound. Reaching the ducks, I was amazed to discover the end of the ramrod had gone through the ice, piercing the head of a twenty pound salmon – I knew it was a twenty pound salmon because it had scales on its back! Stuffing the mallards in my bag, I started to crack the ice to retrieve the fish. I would have fish, flesh and fowl – mission accomplished. Cracking the ice was not a good plan. As I fell into the water, the sharp edges of the ice cut off my head at the neck. I am a fine man in a crisis and grabbing the hair of my own severed head and dipping it in the water, I replaced it back on my neck. Luckily it was cold enough to freeze the head back in place on my neck. I crawled to the shore, being careful to drag the gun and poacher's bag with me.

I made my way home via the rectory, leaving the gun and one mallard in the porch as a measure of my gratitude to the old parson. A tap on the door of our old cottage caused the slightly grumpy retort of 'you're not coming in unless you have got fish, flesh or fowl'. Cockily I snapped that I had all three. The door opened. Shivering, I handed my wife the salmon, always her favourite. To her amazement, this was followed by five wild ducks and a hare. She mellowed a little and invited me in by the fire to warm. By now I had developed a dewdrop on the end of my nose, and wives can never stand that. The warmth from the log fire melted the ice seal around my neck. In the attempt to flick the droplet from the tip of my nose I knocked my own head into the ashes of the fire. Chrissy can usually turn up trumps in a crisis. Grabbing the severed head, she placed it in a bucket and, topping it up with ice, made her way to Ambleside Health Centre. There Dr Birket performed a major piece of microsurgery, replacing my head on my neck just where it remains to this day. However, you must understand I bow rather gingerly at the conclusion of my storytelling performances … just in case.

THE CONEY

This next story is a pre-Darwinian tale, which was gifted to me by 'Scottish Traveller' storyteller Duncan Williamson. In it a very different mammal also struggles with water in its solid state.

Many years ago (before Noah was a sailor), in the vale of Grasmere, there was an animal called a coney. Now the coney was a little bit like a squirrel; he had tiny ears and a big, long, bushy tail. One winter's day, Mr Coney was hopping along the bank of the River Rothay, which is the river that runs under Church Bridge opposite the Storyteller's Garden. He spotted some small trout shining in the stream and wondered how he might catch one for his tea. Who should come stomping down the fell to the riverbank but old Daddy Fox.

'Ah! Mr Coney!' he said. 'I'll show you how to catch a fish!'

He waggled his bottom and flipped the tip of his red tail into the water. He sat patiently waiting for a bite, using his tail as a fishing line. As soon as a fish nipped the end of his tail, he pulled it out gently, seized it in his mouth and strolled back up the fell side to feed the fish to his vixen and cubs.

Mr Coney thought to try the same ploy. He waggled his bottom and flipped the tip of his white tail into the water. He was sat patiently waiting for a bite when who should come slithering upstream but Jack Frost. The river turned to ice, entrapping Mr Coney's tail. He was stuck fast by the tail when who should come flying majestically over the ice but the heron, or as he is known in Lakeland, the Jammy Crane.

Being a friend of Mr Coney, the Jammy Crane paused to help. She seized one of Mr Coney's little ears in her beak, flapped her wings and pulled, stretching the ear. She seized the other ear, flapped her wings and pulled so that Mr Coney's ears were so long that they met over the top of his head. The heron then seized both ears in her beak, flapped her wings and gave an enormous tug. There was a snapping noise as Mr Coney's tail snapped a few inches from his backside, leaving a bobbly tail like a lump of cotton wool.

Confused, Mr Coney shook his head, discovering he had long floppy ears. He looked so different with his long floppy ears and his bobbly tail that all of the other animals stopped calling him Mr Coney and started to refer to him as rabbit or bunny. When in time he fathered young, they too had long ears and bobbly tails and they were called rabbits or bunnies as well.

So it was then and so it is now. However, if anyone ventures to a fur shop (hopefully they wouldn't in this day and age), and if they attempted to buy a coat made of the fur of this animal, the label on the coat will not say rabbit fur; it will say the word coney to remind everyone of this story of how Mr Coney became a rabbit or bunny, a story that a man called Charles Darwin never heard.

STARGAZEY PIE

The story that follows was first told to me in the 1970s by larger-than-life Cornish folk singer Brenda Wooton, who was known across Europe as 'Mama Cornwall'. I remember her singing:

> *A finer place you'd never believe*
> *Than Mousehole on 'Tom Bawcock's Eve'*

The tiny Cornish village of Mousehole stands on the Penryn Peninsula, not far from the larger fishing ports of Newlyn and Penzance. Being as far in the south west of Cornwall as its possible to venture without getting your feet wet, it should not be surprising that tiny Mousehole cops some of the wildest weather that the Atlantic can throw at it!

A couple of hundred years ago, one winter saw particularly bad winds; as the Cornish fisherfolk would say 'It was blowing a hooley'. For the whole of November the gales were so bad that even the weather-hardened Mousehole fisherman couldn't put to sea. Christmas was fast approaching and the families of the fishermen were getting desperate. No fish meant little to eat and no money. In every fishing community there is an 'old salt' who the young bloods look to for the decision about whether it's safe to go to sea. There is also often a stubborn 'old salt' who will go when nobody else dares to venture out of port. At the end of the second week in December, Tom Bawcock stood on the harbour wall and announced to anybody who cared to listen that he would go to sea first light on the morning tide, whatever the weather.

At half-light the next morning there was just one swinging lantern being carried down the steep hill from the dotted fisherman's cottages to the harbour. Tom Bawcock was going to sea! Indeed, he was the only one daring to go to sea. The good people of Mousehole would not go without that Christmas. Even though the wind had eased slightly, it was still blowing a hooley. Tom shot his net. An hour later, when he hauled the net up, he was disappointed to discover in the cod-end of the trawl a selection of the kind of fish that decent Cornish fishermen would use as bait in their crab and lobster pots. Seven different kinds of fish: gurnard, horse mackerel, whiting, a small conger eel, a tiny codling, a baby skate and some Cornish silver darlings – pilchards. Not a great catch, but nevertheless a feed of fresh fish. Like most fishermen, Tom knew well how to prepare and cook this catch. As Tom looked into the basket of fish thoughtfully, an enormous gust of wind and a giant wave knocked him over backward on the slippery deck. As conditions were worsening, Tom decided not to push his luck although he thought it was a pity to head back leaving fish down there in the wet!

Tom moored securely at the tiny quayside and set off up the steep hill with a basket of fish on his back to the cheers of the locals. This was a community who looked after each other and tonight they would all eat. The baker made an extra batch of wholemeal bread and saffron buns. On the way home, Tom borrowed the biggest pie dish in the village from Mrs Tremayne. As soon as he was home he lit his oven and made a large bowl of pastry, rolling it out to line the pie dish. He prepared and cooked up six different kinds of fish, keeping the pilchards and a ball of pastry for the pie's crowning glory.

Making a lid for the pie he cut slits in the lid, pushing a pilchard into each slit with heads and eyes facing up towards the stars (hence the term Stargazey). This was done not for effect, although it did look both strange and magical, but rather so that the rich oil in the heads of the pilchards, the most nutritious and sustaining part of this small fish, could drizzle down and become part of the pie filling. All the villagers crammed into Tom's tiny cottage that night and all ate well for the first time in six weeks.

To this day, in December on Tom Bawcock's Eve (7 December), Mousehole people gather in the pub by the harbour to sing and eat Stargazey Pie in the lead up to the Cornish Christmas.

Tom Bawcock's Song

Written around 1930 by Robert Morton Nance (1873–1959). He based the tune on an old Cornish dance tune called the 'Wedding March'.

A merry plaas you may believe
woz Mowsel pon Tom Bawcock's Eve.
To be theer then oo wudn wesh
to sup o sibm soorts o fesh!

Wen morgee brath ad cleard tha path
comed lances for a fry,
an then us had a bet o scad
an starry gazee py.

Nex cumd fermaads, braa thustee jaads
As maad ar oozles dry,
an ling an haak, enough to maak
a raunen shark to sy!

A aech wed clunk as ealth wer drunk
en bumpers bremmen y,
an wen up caam Tom Bawcock's naam
we praesed un to tha sky.

A merry place, you may believe,
was Mousehole 'pon Tom Bawcock's Eve;
to be there then who wouldn't wish
to sup of seven sorts of fish.

When murgy broth had cleared the path
comed lances for a fry
and then us had a bit o' scad
and starry gazey pie.

Next comed fair maids, bra' thrusty jades
as made our oozles dry
and ling and hake, enough to make
a running shark to sigh.

As each we'd clunk as health were drunk
in bumpers brimming high
and when up came Tom Bawcock's name
we praised him to the sky.

The Farmer's Story

The extreme weather story that follows is from my adoptive home of Cumbria, where the legends grow out of the land. It is unique in the collection in that it is factual. It was formed out of an item on Border Television News and a chance meeting with a local farmer. Sometimes the truth of nature is more remarkable than any fiction.

Shepherds' Song

A man that would a shepherd be, must have a valiant heart
He must not be faint-hearted, but boldly play his part
He must not be faint-hearted, be it hail or wind or snow
For there's no ale on the Fells when the stormy winds do blow.

Traditional

In early 2013, heavy snowfall combined with wild wind storms, creating a desperate time for sheep farmers in West Cumbria, the Isle of Man and parts of Wales. Entire flocks were buried under deep snow for up to two weeks. On the television local news, I was delighted to see hardy sheep being pulled from deep snow, still alive. I noticed, however, that many of the sheep pulled alive from the holes in the snow bank had great chunks of their fleece missing. I wondered why? The following day, chatting to a Lakeland farmer at my local post box, my question was answered. As I waxed lyrical about the marvellous capability of the Herdwick breed, he informed me that the warmth of the sheep's bodies would melt sufficient snow immediately around them to allow them to turn their heads enough to chew off their own wool. Whilst the wool had little value as food, it did have enough natural oil to keep the beast alive for several extra days, hopefully until the rescue came. Now there is a story that is truly remarkable.

A WARM GLOW

As I head into my mid-sixties it is sometimes asked of me what will happen to the stories after I am dead and gone. These written collections will hopefully help to ensure their survival – but what of the skills of oral storytelling? To address this, in recent years as Storytelling Laureate I have taken every opportunity to deliver storytelling training or practical workshop sessions for those who work in education or just interested parents, grandparents or 'would be' storytellers. One or two of these 'would be' storytellers of the future have become mentees or apprentices. These folk absorb both my skills and my repertoire 'learning at the knee' or, as Spike Milligan used to quip, 'at other low joints'.

There comes a time where I point out that if these folk don't give me a story or two in return, then they are reaping the harvest without sowing the seed. One of my mentees brought me the story that follows. Living in my head for a year, I have had just enough dream time to make it my own.

Long ago, in the days when birds built their nests in old men's beards, there was a valley with a scattering of cottages on its fell sides. At the head of the valley stood a great and ancient stone castle. In the cold of winter, the warmest place in this stone edifice was the kitchen, where a great fire glowed. Such was the warmth of this spot that the king and queen willingly sat in this room together, even though it was beneath their station in life.

Sadly a difference grew between the king and queen and they fell out. The fire went out and the queen retreated to her own room in the far tower of the building. Alone, the king also retreated to his own tower down a long draughty corridor far away from the queen. With the fire in the kitchen out, a coldness spread throughout the castle. No matter how hard the servants tried, this fire would not be rekindled. Unstopable, the cold-ness continued to spread and travelled down the valley to the cottages where it chilled the king and queen's subjects, with one exception!

As the midwinter festivities approached, the king summoned his favourite servant and pointed through the slit windows to cottages down the fell side where wisps of smoke curled skywards. The servant was given a lantern and a bag of gold coins and sent to purchase half a dozen red-hot coals to form the heart of a new fire in the castle kitchen. Clad in heavy boots, hat and jacket, the servant set out on his mission. Halfway down the fell, the trusty retainer knocked on the door of the first cottage. The door was opened by a grumpy old man, clearly not pleased at being disturbed. The servant told the curmudgeon that he needed half a dozen red-hot coals to form the heart of a fire in the king's castle. Seeing the moneybag on the servant's belt, the old man told him this would cost twelve pieces of gold. The servant handed over the gold coins in silence and the old man removed six red-hot coals from his fire with tongs and placed them in the lantern. Without a further word passing between them, the servant set off out of the cottage and up the path towards the castle. After just five steps, the coals in the lantern had turned from red to grey. After a further five steps, the coals had turned from grey to black and were so cold that the servant could take them out with his bare hands and toss them into the snow. They were of no use. Mindful of his task, the king's servant walked to the next cottage and knocked on the door. The door was opened by a grumpy old woman. Again the servant informed her he needed six red-hot coals to form the heart of a fire for the king's castle. Seeing the moneybag on the servant's belt, the old woman gave the same response, that this would cost twelve gold coins. The servant shrugged and reached into the bag the king had given him, handing the gold coins over. Wielding the tongs, six red-hot coals were carefully placed in the lantern. Again without conversation the trusty retainer, bearing the lantern, set off towards the castle. Five steps up the lane the red coals had turned grey, and after a further five paces they turned black and cold; indeed so cold that the servant could take them out with his bare hands and toss them into the snow.

Ahead of the servant was just one more tiny cottage with smoke curling up from the chimney. Here the king's servant would experience a different reception. On knocking, the door was opened by a smiling young girl who greeted him warmly. The young lass invited the servant in by the fire and gave him a warming bowl of hot soup. It was the first human kindness the faithful retainer had experienced that day. When he asked for the six red-hot coals for the king's fire the young girl willingly wielded the tongs, placing the glowing coals in the lantern. She then told the visitor that there was one thing she wanted in return. The servant reached for his moneybag. To his surprise she told him that when he reached the castle he had to wish the king and his queen a very Merry Christmas and a happy and peaceable New Year. The servant thanked her and set off up the path towards the castle. After five steps the red-hot coals had got hotter. After a further five paces the coals were so hot that he could barely hold the lantern. Arriving at the castle kitchen, the six red-hot coals were carefully placed to form the heart of a roaring fire. The warm glow spread throughout the castle, reaching the extremities of the towers. The king and the queen ventured down from their solitary retreats and once again sat facing each other in their old seats by the fire. They started talking to each other and in time, as the warmth grew between them, they began to settle their differences. The trusty servant approached them and told them about the smiley young girl who had so freely given them the coals and who had wanted to wish them both a Merry Christmas and a happy and peaceable New Year.

As the warm glow grew, it spread down the valley to the cottages and even mellowed the old man and the old woman. The young girl just smiled knowingly.

PART 2

A LIGHT IN THE MIDST OF DARKNESS

'Christmas is Coming, the Goose is Getting Fat'

Christmas is coming; the goose is getting fat,
Please put a penny in the old man's hat,
If you haven't got a penny, a ha'penny will do,
If you haven't got a ha'penny, God bless you.

Traditional

Room for a Little One

The remarkable Ruth Tongue of Crowcombe in Somerset, whom I had the pleasure of meeting in the 1960s, had heard the following story from a Wincanton farmer's wife in the 1920s. The wife used it to explain the story of the nativity to her children by the fireside as Christmas approached. My own mother had a Somerset accent as rich as hand-churned butter, and my paternal grandmother went into service as a young girl. I draw on my memory of their warmth and voices to tell this story at Christmas. This is a kind of magic that brings a tear to my eye and a smile to my lips simultaneously; I hope that it does the same for all who read it.

Some 2,000 years ago, there was an inn where all the travellers went. The landlord was a big bullish man far too fond of his own ale. He employed a young girl called Bridget from the village to work as a servant. Bridget had to be up at first light to wash the pots, make the beds and serve the breakfast, but, most importantly, she need to make the fires in the great hearths of the inn. To do this she had to go out to Selwood Forest and collect wood, whatever the weather. To make this task a touch easier for a small girl, the landlord gave her a little nirrup – that's a donkey – to carry the logs for the firing. The nirrup slept in a tiny lean-to stable at the back of the inn. It was a small shelter with a battered thatch roof that the stars shone through … but there was 'room for a little one'.

When all the guests and hotel staff were snug in bed, and the landlord lay drink-taken behind the bar, out to the stable Bridget used to run, barefoot. Snuggled up against the donkey's coarse coat she cuddled. There she found enough warmth to sleep a few hours until sunrise. Then, of course, it was back inside to the cleaning and the fires.

One morning Bridget woke up and peeped out of the stable to see a bone-weary, hungry old plough ox, without food or shelter, shivering in the barton. Bridget told the ox she was off to work, so there was 'room for a little one' and a goodish bit of hay in the stable. Somehow the gert ox squeezed in beside the nirrup.

No sooner had Bridget turned up for work, than she was told she would have to take the nirrup and head off to Selwood Forest to collect wood. Off the two of them went; it took them most of the hours of daylight, and when they came back they were both so loaded down with wood you could hardly see their feet, and they looked like blue ice blocks. Bridget loaded the wood by the hearth in the inn and retreated into the stable, beside her new companion the ox.

Then, wouldn't you know it, the master chided Bridget, saying they needed more wood than that. Back to Selwood Forest Bridget would have to go. When he told her, her eyes filled with tears. She had to go out and tell the little nirrup. Bridget told the animals it would be wicked black dark. The nirrup reminded Bridget she had a cross mark on her back to protect them, as indeed all donkeys do, just look. The ox said he would come as well to help. So off the three of them went, through the dark to Selwood Forest.

A bit later, loaded with wood, they started the journey home. There in the moonlight they saw an old man and a woman struggling towards the inn. The woman, heavy with child, needed help. Bridget and the man lifted all the wood on to the ox's back before gently lifting the woman on to the nirrup's back. Off they went, with the old man and Bridget leading. The nirrup was ever so gentle and somehow they seemed to cover the distance quite quickly. In the barton Bridget and the man helped the woman from the nirrup's back and beckoned the couple into the stable. Then Bridget lugged the wood from the ox's back into the inn that was full to the roof-tree with guests. Next Bridget slipped into the pantry and took half a loaf and a hunk of cheese. She had an idea the couple in the stable might be hungry.

When she ran outside one great star shone over the stable, down through the hole in the thatch, and God's dear son was there. There were angels and they were singing. Bridget was singing too. They all shouted out to Bridget who was standing singing, barefoot, in the starshine. They called her to come inside with them, as there was 'room for a little one'.

Bridget turned and went inside, and somehow there was.

The Cherry Tree Carol

Simply one of the most magical traditional carols, the piece that follows tells an apocryphal story that turns edgy as Joseph challenges the idea of the Immaculate Conception. Many English traditional singers have it in their repertoire and it has a place in the Oxford Book of Carols.

Joseph was an old man
And an old man was he,
When he wedded Mary
In the land of Galilee.

Joseph and Mary walk'd
Through an orchard good,
Where was cherries and berries
So red as any blood

Joseph and Mary walk'd
Through an orchard green,
Where was berries and cherries
As thick as might be seen

O then bespoke Mary
So meek and so mild,
'Pluck me one cherry Joseph,
For I am with child.'

O then bespoke Joseph
With words so unkind,
'Let him pluck thee a cherry
That brought thee with child.'

O then bespoke the babe
Within his mother's womb
'Bow down the tallest tree
For my mother to have some.'
Then bow'd down the highest tree
Unto his mother's hand
Then she cried 'See Joseph,
I have cherries at command.'

O then bespoke Joseph –
'I have done Mary wrong:
But cheer up, my dearest,
And not be cast down.'

'O eat your cherries Mary,
O eat your cherries now;
O eat your cherries, Mary,
That grow up on the bough.'

Then Mary pluck'd a cherry
As red as the blood;
Then Mary went home
With her heavy load.

As Joseph was a-walking
He heard an angel sing,
'This night shall be born
Our heavenly king.'

'He neither shall be born
In house nor in hall
Nor in the place of Paradise
But in an ox's stall.'

Traditional

Herod and the Cock

The unusually humorous carol that follows forms the introductory section of a much longer piece describing the Holy Family's flight into Egypt. Yorkshire folk music legends The Watersons sing the whole narrative, but I like to mix song and spoken word. With this in mind I've turned the sequel to the Herod carol, 'The Miraculous Harvest', into a spoken story.

There was a star in David's land,
In David's land appeared;
And in King Herod's chamber
So bright it did shine there.

The Wise Men they soon spied it,
And told the King a-nigh
That a Princely Babe was born that night,
No King shall e'er destroy.

If this be the truth, King Herod said,
That thou hast told me;
The roasted cock that lies in the disk
Shall crow full senses three.

O the cock soon thrusted and feathered well
By the work of God's own hand,
And he did crow full senses three,
In the disk where he did stand.

Traditional

The Miraculous Harvest

As previously stated, this story comes from a carol that forms an episode in the Holy Family's flight from Herod and the Slaughter of the Innocents. There is a glorious fluidity between the twin art forms of narrative song and the spoken word. Song makers often turn told stories into song and we storytellers sometimes turn ballads back to spoken stories.

When the vainglorious King Herod heard that the Christ child had been born – a king far greater than any king who had ever set foot on this earth – he was thrown into a jealous rage. Herod ordered his soldiers to slay the firstborn son of every family in the carnage we have come to call the Slaughter of the Innocents. Jo the old carpenter took his young wife Mary and their newborn baby Jesus and fled to safety.

Some distance down the road they came to a field where a peasant farmer was planting his crop, broadcasting corn seed. Seeing the old man, and the newborn baby in the arms of his mother, the labourer paused in his work and waved to the baby. Excited, the baby waved back, pointing to the field. As the babe pointed to the field the corn seeds sprouted, grew and ripened. In fact the corn ripened so yellow that the farmer could start to harvest it that very day! Joseph saw a cloud of dust getting closer, which he realised to be Herod and his troops with murder on their minds. The proud father and mother hurried down the road to seek safety in a cave. The king and his soldiers halted by the cornfield. They asked the farmer if he had seen an old man and a young woman with a baby. The farmer retorted that he could not tell a lie, as he had seen them. Herod then enquired as to when the peasant had seen them. The farmer then told the king as he continued harvesting his corn that when he had seen the family he had just been sowing the corn seed – which was true of course! Herod reasoned this must have been a season previous and turned his soldiers back to the castle. This allowed the Holy Family to make good their escape into the Holy Land.

The Legend of the Robin

Many years ago an elder – a woman who ran a Sunday school group in a Cornish chapel – gave me the story that follows. Since that day it has remained the most spellbinding and popular of my Christmas tales.

As Joseph, Mary and the baby Jesus were fleeing the carnage wrought by King Herod and his soldiers, which we have come to know as the Slaughter of the Innocents, they sought a safe place to hide. Some way down the road, they spotted a cave in a rocky outcrop. On entering the dark cave, they placed the newborn baby on a rock, where he lay shivering. Joseph knew that if he didn't light a fire the newborn babe would die of the cold. Whilst Mary cuddled the child, Joseph collected a handful of sticks and twigs, the makings of a fire. The old man scrunched up a piece of parchment and, placing it on the cave floor, piled the sticks over it. He put a spark to the parchment and bent down to try and blow the fire into life. Exhausted, and puffing and panting from the journey, the old carpenter was too breathless to manage this task. By chance, a tiny brown bird flew into the cave and hopped over the newborn baby. Seeing the old man struggling with the fire, the tiny bird flapped its wings to help. So enthusiastic were the bird's efforts that the fire flared up suddenly. In fact, the fire flared up so suddenly that it scorched the bird's breast, turning it bright red. Ever since that day this tiny bird has had a red breast, which is why we call him 'Robin Red Breast'.

This is probably why he remains the most popular icon of the Christmas card.

THE LEGEND OF TINSEL

One good story leads to another. It was the telling of 'The Legend of the Robin' that nudged a member of the audience at a Christmas event in my village to tell me the legend that follows. I have since discovered that the Muslim community have virtually the same story about the prophet Mohammed hiding in a cave. It's good to know that two faith communities have common ground in the shape of a magical tale.

Joseph, Mary and the Christ child sheltered by the fire in the cave whilst Herod and his soldiers searched for them, seeking to destroy the child. Jo wished he had enough wood to build a door to keep them safe – despite being a carpenter he had neither wood nor tools with him. A tiny spider played its part in the magic of this moment. The tiny creature zigzagged up and down the cave entrance, trailing its silver thread. By morning, the cave entrance was covered by one enormous cobweb. The morning bought a heavy dew and the web was covered in tiny droplets of water that shone like silver in the morning sunshine. Herod and his troops halted just down the road. One of the soldiers pointed up to the cave, suggesting the family might be hiding there. Herod looked up and saw only the shining silver web. He reasoned no one could be hiding in the cave, otherwise the threads would be broken. Again he turned his soldiers back to the castle, allowing Mary, Joseph and the baby to escape to safety. It's because of the work of this spider that at Christmas we decorate our homes, our Christmas trees or even our hair with the silver threads which we call tinsel.

Ploughing on Christmas Day

Some more puritanical Christians used to have strong opinions about the evils of working on the Sabbath and Christmas Day. This traditional ballad, from the singing of May Bradley from a Shropshire Gipsy family, expresses this belief. In a later story, 'The Apple Tree Man' (see Part 5), one of the brothers states his decision not to work on Christmas Day, although it's not clear whether this is for reasons of religious belief or indolence!

His wife and children's out of place,
His beasts and cattle they're almost lost,
His beasts and cattle they die away,
For ploughing on Old Christmas Day,
His beasts and cattle they die away,
For ploughing on Our Lord's birthday.

A Song for Anyone to Sing

This next song is a nonsense song to be sung at Christmas to the tune of 'I Saw Three Ships'. It shows that the animals of farm, field and forest were not hampered by any of the religious constraints expressed in the 'Ploughing on Christmas Day' ballad.

It is a celebratory song for families to sing together. Have fun with it.

There was a pig went out to dig,
On Christmas Day, Christmas Day,
There was a pig went out to dig
On Christmas Day in the morning.

There was a cow went out to plough,
On Christmas Day, Christmas Day,
There was a cow went out to plough
On Christmas Day in the morning.

There was a doe went out to hoe,
On Christmas Day, Christmas Day,
There was a doe went out to hoe
On Christmas Day in the morning.

There was a drake went out to rake,
On Christmas Day, Christmas Day,
There was a drake went out to rake
In Christmas Day in the morning.

There was a sparrow went out to harrow,
On Christmas Day, Christmas Day,
There was a sparrow went out to harrow
On Christmas Day in the morning.

There was a minnow went out to winnow,
  On Christmas Day, Christmas Day
There was a minnow went out to winnow
  On Christmas Day in the morning.

  There was a sheep went out to reap,
  On Christmas Day, Christmas Day,
  There was a sheep went out to reap
  On Christmas Day in the morning.

  There was a crow went out to sow
  On Christmas Day, Christmas Day,
  There was a crow went out to sow
  On Christmas Day in the morning.

  There was a row went out to mow,
  On Christmas Day, Christmas Day,
  There was a row went out to mow
  On Christmas Day in the morning.

Anon.

The Christmas Goose

The tale that follows is based on an old Yorkshire folk ballad heard by the author from two Yorkshire characters; the first, Derek Elliot from Whitby in North Yorkshire and the second, Will Noble, a singer and dry stone waller from the Holme Valley in West Yorkshire. It probably started life as a barroom yarn before song makers got their hands on it. As a yarn, it was an early example of the genre of humorous stories of randy commercial travellers still to be heard in every inn bar in Britain.

I wish it to be known that Thomas Goodale, the anti-hero of the story, is not known to be a relative of Tom Goodale, the storyteller. I merely borrowed the name – just perfect for a Mancunian purveyor of fine wines and liquor.

> *O good ale though art my darling.*
> *Though art my joy both night and morning*

I'd like to thank the Cumbrian treasure that is Lord Bragg of Wigton for inspiring my version of this story through his novel The Maid of Buttermere *– a great holiday read.*

It was the last knockings of the eighteenth century. In the Vale of Grasmere, Wordsworth, Southey and De Quincy were flexing their quills. In Rydal Hall, as a guest of the Fleming family, a gentle Quaker called William Wilberforce was explaining how he would use his pacifist teeth to chew up the ambitions of young venture capitalists like John Bolton of Storrs Hall, Windermere and Liverpool to build fortunes from the miserable slave trade.

Thomas Goodale, sales representative for a Manchester fine ales and liquor company, was completing 'missionary work' in West Cumbria. He was attempting to convince the gentry of Cockermouth and Workington that there were greater pleasures to be had than locally brewed ale and rum smuggled from slave ships that put into Whitehaven to discharge their sad cargo. It was Christmas Eve and an overnight between Cockermouth and Keswick was necessary on his journey back to the big city.

Accordingly, he rode into the yard of a passable-looking coaching inn – the Pheasant at Bassenthwaite.

As Tom checked in the landlord was excited, as his only son was due to return for Christmas after successfully completing the second year of a law degree at Oxford. Excited though he was, the landlord still had the business acumen to ask whether the traveller would be requiring dinner. As it was Christmas and Goodale's trip had been fruitful, the traveller ordered Christmas goose after a break to settle and wash and change in his room. A couple of hours later, suited and booted, Tom Goodale settled expectantly at a dining table. A bonny servant maid called Betsy duly brought him his dinner on a large silver salver with a domed lid. Goodale smiled at the maid, who tipped him a wink whilst lifting the lid to reveal half a goose drenched in orange sauce, surrounded by crispy roast potatoes and a couple of attendant peeled mandarins and behatted by twists of orange zest.

As the visitor settled to eat he asked the maid if she could deliver some rum and hot water to his room an hour later, the usual sign that she would be expected to perform further duties for his pleasure, normally for financial reward. Smiling, young Betsy undid a blouse button and bobbed a curtsy before disappearing to the back kitchen to take her early evening break.

Full of goose, Goodale returned to his room, where he loosened his galluses and kicked of his boots. Before long there was a gentle tap on the door, which Goodale opened to reveal the blushing Betsy bearing rum and hot water, which she duly placed on the bedside table. The two strangers' arms were soon interlocked and things moved quickly on. The coupling that ensued was as brief as it was unsatisfactory and, Goodale assumed, inconsequential! As the two lay in each other's arms, young Betsy stretched out her hand in the reasonable hope of financial reward. Goodale pressed a golden sovereign into her hand before gracelessly asking for change. Indignant, the chambermaid told him she would give his change when he next returned to the Pheasant. Goodale told her that could be some considerable time hence. The girl assured him she would still be there as her life plans did not involve her moving from the fields, lakes and fells that had given birth to her and shaped her.

Indeed, it was a year to the day before Goodale's rounds took him back to West Cumbria. Arriving back at the coaching inn that was the Pheasant at Bassenthwaite, the traveller found the landlord again excited as his son was returning from Oxford for good on the completion of his three-year law degree. Booking the same room as he did the year before, the traveller again ordered his Christmas goose. An hour later, settling at the dining table, Goodale had mixed feelings when the young servant bringing him the domed silver salver was the same Betsy the chambermaid, who bobbed a curtsy with a wry smile. Tom lifted the domed lid to reveal not a goose, but a bonny baby boy! Blushing, Tom Goodale enquired as to the meaning of this. Betsy told him that a year previous when he'd paid her a sovereign for her services, he had demanded his change. It was this change that she now brought him … on a plate.

The traveller went straight to the bar, cancelled his room, settled his bill and left for home. Betsy settled down to proudly bring up her young son as best she could.

Her situation improved when the landlord's son came to realise her beauty, strength of character and appetite for work. He started to 'walk out' with her. This relationship developed and, after several years, led to marriage, with the young son proudly giving his mother away.

Before many more years the old landlord died and the Pheasant passed on to the son, his wife and stepson. They immediately ceased trading with the Manchester fine wine and liquor company, instead switching to a reputable Carlisle company. This meant that Thomas Goodale had no necessity to ever set foot in that valley again and was soon forgotten.

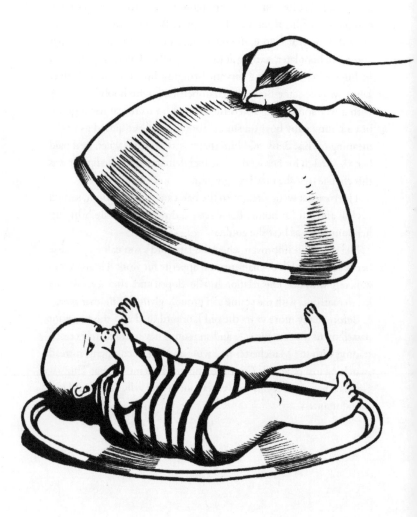

Trefor's Turkey

Jim Rees, an expatriate Welshman, lived much of his life in Grasmere in the English Lake District with his wife Vivienne. Whenever necessary, he put me right on my Welsh pronunciation in stories (something he enjoyed!), for his years never diluted his Welshness! After his death his widow passed on the story that follows, telling me that Jim drew on the smells and fond memories of the Swansea market of his boyhood. If I haven't remained true to this story, a ghost may attack me from the rear and smack me over the head with a leek.

Trefor Jones, or 'Jones the Turkey', to give him his nickname in the Mumbles, ran a small farm rearing the finest turkeys in the Vale of Glamorgan. As Christmas approached he donned the bloody apron and retreated to a small wooden shed where, both night and day, throats were slit, feathers plucked and innards drawn. This done, the illustrious farmer called at the wash house, a lean-to next to the back door of his small slate-grey farmhouse overlooking his fifty or sixty acres of scrubby land. Retiring in his armchair with a pint mug of strong, sweet tea, he patiently waited for his efforts to bear fruit. He cheered himself with the fact that others, namely his cousins Megan and Guto, would be the ones charged with manning the turkey stall in the cold of winter selling the corpses of the birds to a mixture of housewives and hotel chefs, an onerous task for which Trefor paid them a pittance.

One year, as Christmas approached, Megan and Guto contacted Trefor with the news that they were both suffering from a bad dose of influenza. The main Christmas market was fast approaching and Trefor realised that, exhausted though he was from preparing the turkeys, he would have to turn out and take care of the stall alone. Wouldn't you just know it; it was freezing 'an inch an hour'. As Trefor stood shivering at the stall, on his right was the cockles and laverbread stall and all around blazing buckets of fire to warm the cockles of the shoppers' hearts (this was in the days before risk assessment). Thankfully, in front of him was the tea and soup stall. On this day of the year only, this stall also boasted the finest mince pies in Wales, displayed in a position usually occupied – for the other fifty-one weeks of the year – by the finest Welsh cakes in Wales. Trefor's turkeys sat dissolutely in pink regimented rows and aided by his dour sales patter, in both English and Welsh, gradually disappeared into the voluminous bags of excited mothers and grandmothers, until only one remained. Trefor stood resolute, determined not to return home with just one unsold bird. Coming through the crowd towards him, our hero spotted a pompous woman, as Jim used to say, 'All red hat and no drawers'. She eyed the remaining turkey before pronouncing that it didn't 'fit the bill' as it was too small. Seizing the bird, Trefor whisked it round to the back of the stall, where he slightly rearranged the carcass, tucking a small green bunch of fresh parsley under each wing.

Returning, he proudly placed the same bird, now sporting its new adornment, in front of the woman with the red hat. She smiled and confirmed that this bird would be just perfect. Trefor's delight was only ruined when she told him that she was so pleased, she would take both that one and the first one she had been shown!

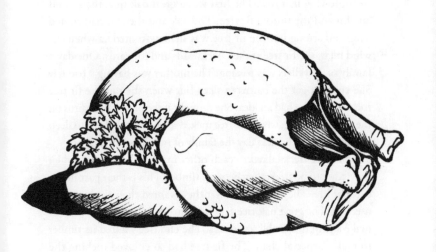

THE THREE TREES

My friend, storyteller and songwriter Bob Pegg, gave me the bones of the story that follows several years ago. It has changed in my hands, and I have discovered that there are other versions where one of the trees forms the wood for the Cross. My version, however, is a magical Christmas story.

Two thousand years ago in the north of England, there were three trees growing in a row. The first was a great oak tree, the second an elm and the third a fir tree. The oak and the elm had rooted deep and strong but the fir tree was shallow-rooted so when the wind blew, the fir tree rocked backwards and forwards. One day a family of Travellers was passing. The mother was having a bad day. She couldn't get the bairns to sleep but when she saw the fir tree rocking that she had an idea. She thought if she placed the bairns on the root of the tree, when the tree rocked it would rock them to sleep, and it worked! The next day the family of travellers travelled on.

The three trees talked to each other for trees know that, when they cease to be trees, they become timber. This is their part in the cycle of life. They talked of what they wanted their timber to be used for. The great oak tree said it wanted its planks to be used to make a ship to sail the seven seas. The elm tree wanted its timber to make a special chair. The fir tree had so enjoyed rocking the bairns to sleep that it wanted its timber to be used to make a cradle.

Three days later men came with axes and saws and felled and planked the three trees.

There was sufficient timber from the great oak tree to make not one, not two, but three ships to sail the seven seas. This Christmas you may sing a carol about these three ships.

The fine-grain timber from the elm went to make a chair for the travelling storyteller, and it is this chair that the storyteller sits on to tell his stories.

The wood from the fir tree was knotted and gnarled and such poor quality that it was just slung into a yard. There it stayed until a Lakeland farmer with an eye for a bargain bought it and had it fashioned into a coarse pinewood box, which was thrown into his byre, where it gradually filled with hay and straw. There it stayed until an old carpenter and his pregnant wife came to sleep the night in that byre. That night, when the wife gave birth to a boy, the baby was placed in this rough pinewood box of hay.

So you see, the wood from that fir tree came to make a very special cradle, and I like to think that it's because of this story that, in a corner of almost every building in this country at this time of year, you'll find a small decorated fir tree – the one we call our 'Christmas Tree'.

The Three Trees Poem

After the following poem was sent to me by Orton WI stalwart and writer Jackie Huck, one of my musician friends, Tony Farren, realised it fitted perfectly to the tune of the traditional song 'John Barleycorn'. Nowadays, whenever Tony and I perform together around Christmas, I tell the story and he follows it with the sung poem. My thanks to both.

An oak, an elm and a waving fir
Sang 'neath a summer sky.
'What will you be,' asked the southern wind,
'When the axe-man chances by?'

'I'll be a ship,' said the oak with pride,
'And surge through a stormy sea,
Sailors will know that I'm safe and strong
And put their trust in me.'

'I'll be the love in a craftsman's hands,'
Said the elm, 'as he shapes with care
My sturdy wood into faithful friends,
A cupboard or a chair.'

But the fir remembered a gypsy babe
She'd rocked in a gentle arm,
Stilled his cries through a Winter's night
And guarded him from harm.

'I'll be a cradle,' the fir tree said,
'And rock to a baby's sighs,
Sharing dreams, soothing fear,
Watched by an angel's eyes.'

So the axe-man came and felled the trees,
With a Chop! Chop! Chop! They fell,
But would their wishes for afterlife
Come true? Only fate would tell.

The oak was made into three fine ships,
That sailed on a Christmas morn,
Bearing tidings to all the world,
That a precious child was born.

The elm became a comfy chair
Where a Story-Teller spun
His tales of timeless magic,
Bringing joy to everyone.

But the toppled fir with its knotted grain
Became just a box of pine,
Left in a stable filled with straw
For ox and ass to dine,

Until the night when a carpenter
And his dear wife came to call,
When the fir-tree manger proved to be
The finest tree of all.

Jackie Huck

The Christmas Cat

Just before Christmas 2009, I was in the Storyteller's Garden in Grasmere when an elderly lady arrived. My visitor told me the welcome news that she had come to tell me a story. As is our custom, a cup of tea or 'chatter watter' was produced. She told me that she loved stories and hailed from the small Gloucestershire village of Uley. This interested me even more as Uley had been the home of my paternal grandmother, Sarah Fisher. The lady assured me that members of the Fisher family still lived in that village. Refreshed by the tea, she proceeded to recount the story that follows, telling me she told it every year at the village school.

Since it has become part of my repertoire, it has been embraced and used by many of my clergy friends. Indeed, after one of my sessions with the Durham Diocese, a canon of Durham Cathedral told me that I might have just solved the problem of a story for his Christmas Eve sermon. I love to think of the choir and congregation mooing along. If you want to tell the story for Christmas, the tune is 'Away in a Manger'.

When children pray, they say, 'Gentle Jesus, Meek & Mild'. However, according to this story, the Christ child was not meek and mild: he was a naughty, naughty boy!

At the first Christmas the newborn lay in his rough firwood cradle, screaming and wailing. His mother Mary had a problem – someone had to sing a lullaby and she had a sore throat. Next to her was her husband Joseph. Well, he didn't normally sing ... and when he did, he didn't sing normally!

The animals gathered around, realising they would have to help.

The cows cleared their throats and struck up with:

This just made the baby cry even louder.

The sheep decided they would try and help:

Baa   baa baa   baa__   baa baa baa__   baa baa baa baa

Again, the baby cried even louder. A tiny black cat walked into the stable – well, actually a black and brown cat, for on its way it had stepped in several cowpats and sheep droppings. Puss offered to lend her voice. The other animals pointed out that she was far too dirty to approach the baby Jesus and that she should go down to the beck and wash herself. The cat turned and walked down to the stream. It took so long for the cat to get herself clean that by the time she returned the baby had cried himself to sleep, as babies do.

The cat walked up to the crib and announced loudly that she would sing. Mary, Joseph and all the other animals uttered a loud SHUSHHHH, as the baby was asleep. The cat, however, complained in a sad little voice that she would really like to sing to the newborn. Mary promised that if ever her baby needed a lullaby in the future, it would be the cat's turn to sing it, provided she kept herself clean. Ever since that day, every pussycat on earth has kept itself spotlessly clean. I have no idea whether a cat ever got to sing its lullaby to the baby Jesus, but if it did it will have sounded something like this:

Meaow meaow meaow meaow__ meaow meaow meaow__ meaow meaow meaow meaow

OFFSIDE!

The Christmas fraternisation of 1914 is well known, thanks to the letters and diaries of the soldiers who were part of it. I have tried to use my years of total immersion in oral storytelling to present Christmas 1914 in the tale that follows.

In December 1914, the soldiers of the king under the command of General Haigh were locked in battle with the troops of Kaiser Wilhelm II on a long front across Flanders – sometimes in France, more often in Belgium. This was especially sad, as many of the brave young men who had joined up had done so believing it would be all over by Christmas.

Rather than this, at the blast of an officer's whistle the men went 'over the top' from their trenches to be scythed down by a hale of bullets from across no-man's-land in the attempt to gain a minute piece of land that would often revert back to the opposition in the battle the following day with a similarly catastrophic loss of life.

In the peace of his office in the Vatican City, Pope Benedict XV suggested a temporary hiatus in the war for the celebration of Christmas. Around the large circular tables of their respective command centres, the high-ranking German and British officers had no appetite for this. By now they had just managed to get their men so well trained that they would undertake almost any task when ordered, no matter how hopeless and suicidal the mission. It seems, nonetheless, that even though the officers and politicians were unable to build up the appetite for peace that the Pope wished to feed, as Christmas drew nearer along the trenches – and men received Christmas parcels from loved ones at home – the warmth of the Christmas spirit was growing.

A rash of tiny fir trees broke out in no-man's-land. Some of the Germans reached over the top of their trenches to wrench them up, replanting them in the piles of earth that marked the edge of their trench. On Christmas Eve, the Germans illuminated these trees with candles. Fifty yards opposite, across the shell holes and abandoned dead bodies of no-man's-land, a Bedfordshire regiment paused to open their parcels from home. Tommy and Billy, two mates who had met at trials for Luton Town FC, a League team, just before going together to the army office to sign up, were opening their parcels from home. Tommy had a knitted blanket, a fruitcake and cigarettes, or 'coffin nails', as they called them. Billy was amazed to discover that his father had sent him a caser, a brown flattened leather football filled with a pink rubber bladder with the nozzle pointing through the lace holes. Tommy and the other soldiers pulled his leg. Why would his dad think he would need this? Billy couldn't resist blowing it up immediately, using a small piece of twig to seal the tube. As no officers were at hand, Billy and Tommy started a game of 'Keepy Uppy'. This was ended only by an outbreak of singing from the German trench:

Stille nacht
Heilige nacht

The English soldiers responded:

Silent night
Holy night

Truly remarkable, two nations singing the same carol to each other in the middle of a war. Then the fraternisation began in earnest. After a friendly – if confused – interchange of shouts, both sides climbed out of their trenches, not with guns but with spades. Brief and rather formal handshakes followed before they set to respectfully burying their dead, who had been laying there for weeks, if not months. Billy hadn't been able to resist bringing his new present – the brown leather caser – with him to show the others. Gerhart, a German infantry man who prior to the war had played as goalkeeper for Bayern Munich, suggested a game of 'Fussbal'.

Up until this point both sides were still wearing their metal helmets, removing them only briefly for the burials of their dead. Now, helmets were off, two pairs of them placed to delineate goals. Stripped of protective headwear, this was not just a game of football, but a game of trust. Tommy dribbled down the wing before centring the ball to Billy, who was just about to score when Gerhart screamed 'offside', seizing the ball and booting it downfield to a team member, who tapped it into goal. After a short while the precious ball was accidentally booted into a roll of barbed wire where, with a hissing sound, it expired. This signalled the end of the sporting engagement. Both sides shook hands and returned to their respective trenches. A few minutes later, a sharp blast form an officer's whistle and the crash of a 'whiz bang' shell started the whole sorry mess again. Billy's first shot over the parapet wounded Gerhart. Billy couldn't resist shouting 'that wasn't offside, was it'. Although he immediately felt guilty for the cheap line, the burst of laughter that followed from both trenches was one of the last normal social interchanges between the two groups of young men for a further four years. As for the football, it can be argued that wasn't settled for a further forty years until 1966 at Wembly!

William and the Bull

*In times past – before just about every church boasted an organ –
remote, rural parishes relied on a choir to provide the music and the
congregation sang along with an often random band of musicians
with crumhorns, viols and serpents, often seated in the west gallery
of the church. The oddities and varied talents of these loyal custodians
of the English church music tradition were well documented by the
likes of Thomas Hardy whose grandfather, a fiddler, played in such
a band. This story is inspired by every musician who made it to the
west gallery, at times with a hangover, and my friend, Dorset musician
Tim Laycock, himself a paragon of sobriety.*

The following poem by Thomas Hardy informs the story:

The Oxen

Christmas Eve, and twelve of the clock.
'Now they are all on their knees,'
An elder said as we sat in a flock
By the embers in hearthside ease.

We pictured the meek mild creatures where
They dwelt in their strawy pen,
Nor did it occur to one of us there
To doubt they were kneeling then.

So fair a fancy few would weave
In these years! Yet, I feel,
If someone said on Christmas Eve,
'Come; see the oxen kneel,

'In the lonely barton by yonder coomb
Our childhood used to know,'
I should go with him in the gloom,
Hoping it might be so.

Thomas Hardy

William the fiddler led his gallant village band with skill and enthusiasm, whether it be in the village hall for a barn dance or in the west gallery of the church, above the stern eye of the parson, for Sunday services. Advent was a particularly busy time for this enthusiastic group. Every Friday, Saturday, and some weekday evenings, occasioned a country dance in the parish hall, arranged by the various local groups and societies.

As Christmas approached, William and the band were exhausted, but so busy that at least there was no need to practise. The last dance of the season, in fact the last dance of the year, was always on Christmas Eve. William and the others drew on their last resources of stamina, with a parish hall packed to the rafters. It was 'Up the Sides and Down the Middle'.

Up the Sides and Down the Middle

Many times the head couple reached the top of the set and handed William a glass of cider. It would have been churlish of him not to accept the gift and slosh it back. The next time through the dance, when the top couple reached William, they gave him a large whisky. He was mixing his drinks …

As the evening drew to a close, William was droozled with drink. As his head was muddled, he decided to take the short cut home from the hall to his tiny cottage across Farmer Merryweather's fifteen-acre field. However, because of the drink, our hero had forgotten the one notable inhabitant of that field: Farmer Merryweather's prize-winning Hereford bull. William had just reached the middle, as far as he could be from the five-bar gates on either side, when he was deafened by the stamping of hooves. He was engulfed in a cloud of steam. In the middle of this cloud there were two eyes burning like red coals and a gold ring shining through a nose – the bull!

William didn't panic. He assessed the situation and realised there was no way he could make it to either gate before feeling the points of the bull's horns in his bottom. He did the only thing that

a musician could do in this situation. He took out his fiddle and
started to play the 'Dorset Triumph'.

Dorset Triumph

To William's delight the pounding hooves ceased and the
bull started to nod its head to the music in perfect time. Farmer
Merryweather's bull was the music critic for the *Farmer's Weekly*!
William realised that as long as he continued to play the fiddle he
was safe, though any attempt to move from the spot was instantly
detected. For a matter of hours he played every country dance
tune in his not-inconsiderable repertoire. However, he eventu-
ally reached the point he was dreading when he had played every
dance tune he knew. He realised he couldn't just start at the beginning again, for if the bull was that much of a connoisseur, it would
know. Silence fell over the field, and then the pounding hooves
and the steam recommenced. The eyes burned redder and brighter.
In desperation, William dredged the depths of his musical memory
and decided to start playing tunes from his repertoire of sacred
music. He struck up with 'All Things Bright and Beautiful'.

Working through his knowledge of church music, he played
everything he knew, finishing with 'Abide with Me'.

Abide with Me

As all fell silent, the hooves and the steam started again with even more ferocity. A spark lit in William's memory and he launched into the nativity carol, 'While Shepherds Watched Their Flocks by Night'.

While Shepherds Watched Their Flocks by Night

The bull cocked up its ears, recognising the tune at exactly the time the church clock struck midnight – it was Christmas. The hooves stopped pounding, the steam cleared and the bull reverently lowered itself to the grass in a kneeling position. As soon as the bull had settled, William, still playing the tune, started to stroll towards the gate. The stroll became a trot, and the trot became a sprint, and by the time William reached the gate he was running faster than Usain Bolt while playing the violin. Landing on the safe side of the gate, William used the tip of his fiddle bow to raise his cap and wished the bull a very merry Christmas.

Then for William it was home, a quick wash, change and a bowl of porridge, before he made his way to the west gallery of the ancient church to join his loyal, if hung-over, band mates. Sure enough, the first tune the parson called for was 'While Shepherds Watched'. William just smiled and wondered if the bull was still kneeling in the middle of the field.

Down't Lonnin

The following piece was gifted to me by the late Joyce Withers of Grasmere. Folk knew that Christmas had arrived when they heard her wonderful telling of it at the annual Christmas readings.

Down t' lonnin' they came,
Just Braithwaite's Mary with Joe, that she wed Lammas year,
And their li'le lad in her arm.

Moon was low and clear
Above Silver How, and mists writhin' up from t'lake,
And light sharp and silver, as 'tis
Of a winter dusk with the night beginning to break
On the darkening dale.

There were no mysteries
Round Mary and Joe; they smiled at us, going by –
'Grand evening!' Joe called out, and Postie said 'Aye!'
And our Libby, she ran to set them a bit on road,
As Mary turned, and showed
T'bairn sleeping soft and warm …

Up Huntingstile
They went; and the young moon dropped over Silver How,
And the night shut down; and now
We saw them no more; their footsteps after a while
Died into mists and darkness.

Up lonnin' they came
Late in the evenin'; we never heard them come,
Though night was still
As a sheltered tarn is – only a whisper from
The li'le beck near at hand, splashin' down in spate.
Quiet they came, and late,
And none said owt as they passed us – just so.

A young lass, walking wearily, and a man ... like Joe
... Or not so like, maybe? ... and the two of 'em bent
Over a bairn asleep; and as they went
Through the dark trees and lake mists, there was light.
Up t'lonnin they came,
Just Braithwaite's lass wi' her man, on a winter's night –
Just Braithwaite's Mary – who else? – in the Christmas night.

Anon.

PART 3
RIDDLE ME,
RIDDLE ME, RANDY~O

'What can promote innocent mirth,
and I may say virtue, more than a good riddle?'

George Eliot, Middlemarch

Introduction

Riddles have long been a vibrant part of the surviving oral tradition of the British Isles. It's probably the sheer challenge of tackling a puzzle presented to you by a loved one. Three friends are necessary for a riddle to function. Firstly there is the riddler who has the knowledge; secondly there is the wise listener who can either solve the riddle or wishes to know the answer. However, for maximum comedy impact (and the oral tradition is a social art), a third person who fails to solve the riddle is required. Riddles include a rich element of teasing (though hopefully non-malicious): even as a boy growing up in the 1950s in a semi with no television, I recall my father teasing me that if I was to make my way in the world, I had to know how many beans make five. The answer of course is:

A bean and a half,
And a half bean,
A bean and a quarter,
And a quarter bean,
A half a bean,
And a whole bean.

Armed with this priceless information, I have made my way through the world as teacher, fisherman and professional storyteller!

Other childhood memories of riddles bring back thoughts of Christmas, and with Christmas came crackers, every one containing a riddle on a slip of paper next to the paper hat. For example,

What is black and white
And red (read!) all over?

This showed me that there are a whole string of riddles that only really work orally.

In my student years I recall a craze for lateral thinking puzzles – these are merely riddles with intellectual pretence:

☙

Puzzle A

A man with a pack on his back was heading towards a field. He knew when he reached the field he would die. Why?

Puzzle B

Romeo and Juliet lay dead in a damp patch on the floor surrounded by a circle of broken glass. Felix sloped out through the door with his head down, knowing he was in trouble.

This second puzzle is especially interesting because it's also a tiny story. There are many traditional tales where the entire story is a riddle or, more commonly, where the protagonists have to solve a riddle or riddles to save themselves – the Stanhope Fairies (published in Taffy's Coat Tales*) and the Star-Apple (published as part of the storytelling Young Heritage project – '3 Golden Apples') are fine examples of these from my own repertoire.*

Two riddle stories follow this next series of short riddles. If you are confounded, don't despair; the answers to all the riddles are in the 'In Conclusion' story at the end of the book. My one clue to help you along is that the first two riddles have the same answer. Good luck!

Riddle 1

Riddle me Riddle me Randy-O
My mother gave me some seeds to sow
The seeds were black and the ground was white
Riddle me Riddle me Randy-O

What is it?

Riddle 2

Flour of England, fruit of Spain
Met together in a shower of rain;
Put in a bag, tied round with a string;
If you tell me this riddle
I'll give you a ring.

What am I?

Riddle 3

I'm called by the name of a man,
Yet am as little as a mouse;
When Winter comes I love to be
With my red target near the house.

What am I?

Riddle 4

I've got six arms
I can swallow whole farms,
Yet a million can become a man.

What am I?

Riddle 5

Your greedy friend, by your side my place I make,
I'll eat anything you feed to me, but a drink I'll never take.

What am I?

Riddle 6

I am black and much admired,
Men hunt me until they're tired.
I've tired ponies and I've tired men,

What am I?

Riddle 7

Highty, tighty, paradighty,
Clothed all in green,
The king could not read it,
No more could the queen;
They sent for the wise men
From out of the East,
Who said it had horns,
But was not a beast.

This is a very old riddle or nursery rhyme.
What is it?

Three Mince Pies

This old riddle story probably started its life in the Middle East as a tale about two fathers and two sons fishing. They only caught three fish yet they each had a whole fish for their supper!

I recently heard it from a teenager in Liverpool about two mothers, two daughters and burgers! In the interests of seasonality, I made it into a riddle story about mince pies.

It was getting near to Christmas, the decorations were beautiful and the Christmas shoppers were freezing and hungry. The baker's shop window was steamed up but the pastries displayed looked irresistible ...

Two mothers and two daughters went into a bakery and bought ONLY three mince pies. They took them home and each ate a whole mince pie.

How is this possible?

Horse Play

The tricky riddle story that follows I first heard from storytelling friends from London. In my hands it has become informed by memories and the culture of my West Country farming upbringing. I have also discovered that versions of this riddle tale are alive and well in Bradford's Islamic community. There it appears as a story about a king and his sons, two princes. It is also noticeable that the wise woman who aids the sons in my West Country version is replaced by a wise man ... usually the Mullah, thus the two variants express the diversity of the two cultures, a mixture of contrast and common ground.

There was once a farmer who had a fine farm and two equally fine young sons. Both sons saw their futures as farmers on the land inherited from their father. They had worked hard on the farm that year and, as Christmas approached, their father felt they deserved something special for their efforts. Soon the Christmas season was upon them and the large farmhouse boasted a fifteen-foot high Christmas tree beautifully decorated with antique glass globes and tinsel with a star on top. As both parents and sons gathered under the tree on Christmas morning, after their traditional breakfast of pork pie and piccalilli, there was a cluster of presents under the tree with the two sons' names on them but they didn't appear to be anything substantial. The young men had been looking forward to something a little extra this year and plucked up the courage to ask their father, who was not a mean man, if anything was wrong. Dryly he beckoned for them to follow him to the barn, where he showed them two ponies, a chestnut and a grey. These were the sons' very special Christmas presents from their parents. Excited, they saddled the shining lithe horses, leading them to the meadows where they raced them. This sibling sport provided so much pleasure that they repeated it daily. This was not always with the total approval of the father, who needed a little more work from them.

The farmer was in the autumn of his years; the time was approaching when he might die. He had a problem, for there is a saying in farming communities 'where there's a will, there's a family'. He knew he had to devise a way to decide which of the two lads would inherit the farm. He wrote a will that said that on the day he was buried, the two sons were to take the two horses to the meadows and race them – the one whose horse came last would inherit the farm. In short, he had left them a riddle.

Safe in the knowledge he had made his decision, he took to his bed and, a few weeks later, he peacefully passed away. The following day the two sons took their father's coffin to the churchyard and laid him in the ground … full of tears. They then returned to the farmhouse for a ham sandwich and the reading of the will. There was a tension, as neither brother knew who would be their father's choice for the land he'd nurtured and treasured for the whole of his working life. The family lawyer did nothing to calm things when he informed the lads that their father had left them a riddle to make the decision.

The will told them they had to take the horses to the meadows and race them … the one whose horse came last would then inherit the farm. The two sons glanced at each other and looked mystified. They thought it best to carry out their father's wishes, though, so they saddled the ponies and led them to the meadow to a fence post they used as start and finish. They winked at each other and mounted as the lawyer shouted 'on your marks, get set, go!' Neither would move hoof nor hair. They sat as the seconds became minutes, as the minutes became hours; in fact, they were still stationary as the daylight began to fade. They knew they needed help. From their positions atop the ponies they both faced each other and simultaneously uttered the words 'the Henwife'.

In the village there was a slightly strange wise woman known to all the villagers as the Henwife. She was the one who assisted the midwife or even acted as midwife at the birth of every baby in that remote community. At the other end of the villagers' lifespans she laid out the bodies on kitchen tables, closing the sightless eyes of the deceased and placing silver coins upon their eyelids. The two farm lads dismounted, tying their ponies to the post, and set off together to the Henwife's remote cottage. They knocked on the door and a strange squeaky voice instructed them to enter. The old woman was seated by the fire with a large white hen on her lap. With one hand, the woman stroked the hen and with the other she stroked her chins. Gently she gave the lads her condolences at this sad time, for she knew their father to be a decent sort. When she enquired as to how she might help, they explained the problem of the riddled will. The wise woman smiled knowingly, thought for a moment and then uttered just two words. As soon as she said these two words the boys thanked her and, leaping up, raced out of the cottage and off to the meadow. They leapt on the horses and started to ride like the wind until one triumphed over the problem their father had set them.

So my riddle is, what were the two words the Henwife uttered? It was only two words and if you are mystified, the answer is on the final page of this book.

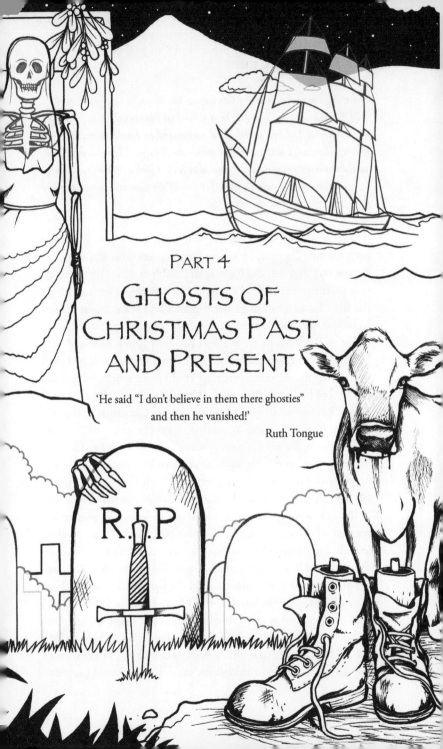

PART 4

GHOSTS OF
CHRISTMAS PAST
AND PRESENT

'He said "I don't believe in them there ghosties"
and then he vanished!'

Ruth Tongue

R.I.P

The Poacher's Curse

The story that follows is my Christmas version of a tale given to me by a 10-year-old Italian girl in a school in Nantwich, Cheshire, in the 1980s. All of her family had emigrated to England except her grandfather, who was too old to make the change. This was his story and the youngster treasured it and kept it as a link to the distant elder, because storytelling can do that. It's one of my favourite ghost stories because of the twist in the tale.

It was before my time, before your time, but it was in somebody's time. There was a young farm worker who was so poor that he was starving, and his wife and children they were starving too. As if that wasn't bad enough, Christmas was approaching, the time for families to gather together and feast: it was going to be lean pickings for this tiny family. The thing that made it worse was that, as he went about his daily grind, he could see his master's pheasants roosting in the trees. He knew if he took just one of those plump birds, he could cook a rich broth that would feed his family for a week. Although pheasant broth is not a great Christmas dinner, it's better than no Christmas dinner at all. The young man also knew that, if caught, the punishment for poaching the master's game was death by hanging. He felt, however, that his duty to his wife and two kids was greater than his duty to his master. He waited for a dark foggy night, then left his tiny cottage with a lantern and a snare – a wire noose on a stick. He went quietly to a tree where he knew the pheasants roosted – he'd seen them there silhouetted like commas on the branch. He slipped the snare up the trunk of the tree and round the neck of a fine cock pheasant. Immediately the pheasant was flapping around in the noose, just as the farm worker was to flap around in a noose before the end of my tale! He lowered the stick and, removing the game bird from the snare, he quickly and cleanly killed it instantly by snapping its neck. He stuffed the bird under his coat and turned home to the safety of his tiny cottage. Walking through the door, he discovered his wife and children had trimmed the small fir tree in the corner of the kitchen with tinsel and candles. He sat down with a waste bin, plucking the feathers from the pheasant ready for the pot. He quickly and effortlessly drew the bird and was just plotting the recipe for the broth when there was an ominous knock on the door. In the Christmas holiday, a policeman on duty was the last person the poor farm labourer expected to see. There was no time to hide the pheasant carcass. The policeman told the young man he was charged to appear in the local courtroom as soon as it reconvened the day after Twelfth Night. It was hardly a relaxing Yuletide for the young man, his wife and family with that hanging over their heads. The officer of the law, a local man, was at least sufficiently aware of their poverty to leave them the pheasant, so even though they were frightened over Christmas, at least they weren't starving.

On 6 January, the young man was marched into the local court before the judge. The public gallery was full, as many of the villagers had committed the same crime and wanted to see how the young man fared. The judge looked around the court and saw a room full of folk that he thought needed teaching a lesson. He reached under the bench for the black cap, a small square of black cloth that told everyone he was about to pronounce the death sentence. The young man gripped the bar in front of him till his knuckles turned white, while the judge found him guilty of poaching the master's game and instructed him that he would be taken to a place of execution to be hanged until he was dead. As he was marched from the courtroom to his doom, he held his head high, for he still thought he had done right for his wife and his children. Leaving the court he passed through a room full of folk no better and no worse than himself, so he crooked a finger and cursed them, foretelling that he would return twelve months to the day and haunt them. He was then taken to a place of execution and hung by the neck until he was dead. His body was laid to rest beneath the big yew tree in the village churchyard.

That night, all the villagers gathered in the local pub and raised a glass to the memory of the young man who died so bravely to save

his family. The main talk, however, was of his curse. The locals decided they would meet twelve months to the day and drink again to his memory and hopefully lay his ghost to rest.

So it was that the following January they met to drink to his memory. On this occasion there was a stranger in the bar – a traveller passing through, a braggart, a boastful man. He enquired as to the story of the poacher's curse, so the locals told him the story, just as I have told you. The stranger laughed 'Ha!' – he didn't believe in ghosts. He bet everyone in the bar he would go to the poacher's grave at midnight, as he had no fear of ghosts. The locals shook hands on the bet but they had a problem – how would they know if he had fairly won or lost? Certainly none of them planned to venture as far as the church-yard at midnight – they all did believe in ghosts and the power of a condemned man's curse. The braggart told them he had a plan to solve this problem: in his belt he carried a knife and, at the first stoke of midnight from the old church clock, he would pull out the knife and stick it in the grass on top of the poacher's grave – proof that he had been there. All decided this was fair and the wager was on! As the clock in the pub reached half past eleven, the stranger wrapped his cloak – a black ankle-length worsted wool cape – around himself and set off for the church-yard. Arriving there in the dim starlight, he stood with one foot on each side of the grave. With the first stroke of midnight, he whipped out the knife and stuck it in the turf on top of the grave. But, just then, he heard a noise behind him. Fearing it was indeed the ghost, he turned to run away … but could not move. Scared stiff, he believed the ghost had him fast by the ankles and, in shock, he suffered a heart attack and fell dead across the grave. When the villagers arrived at the graveyard with the first light of morning, they found the corpse of the braggart lying across the poacher's grave. His knife was indeed sticking in the grave top, although before piercing the grass, the knife had gone through the hem of the ankle-length black cloak. It was that which had rooted him to the spot. Some folks will tell you the noise behind him had truly been the ghost.

Others will tell you the sound was just the wild winter's wind rustling through the great branches of the great yew tree. You and I will never know.

The two ghost stories that follow have been previously published in my Cumbrian Folk Tales *collection by The History Press. They make a guest appearance in this collection because they are seasonally specific.*

THE CHESS PUZZLE

This is a Cumbrian variant of 'The Vanishing Hitchhiker', an urban myth that exists throughout the UK and the USA. The amount of detail is what gives the story its credence; it's the fact that in the 1950s only the intrepid would drive over bleak Shap Fell in the middle of winter on a black starless night that gives the tale its verity. I think I was told it on a dark night at the bar of a remote pub.

On Christmas Eve 1957, a commercial traveller was making his way home to spend Christmas with his family from the Deep South, Stockport, travelling up the A6 heading for Carlisle. It was a dark, starless night and the farther north he journeyed, the more the weather worsened. As he passed through the village of Shap, on that bad bend by the churchyard, he spotted a shadowy figure thumbing a lift. As it was Christmas and a foul night, he stopped to pick up the hitchhiker after discovering he too was heading for Carlisle. As they travelled north, they struck up a conversation to help shorten the journey. The driver discovered the hitchhiker was a retired milkman called Ken and that they had a common passion for the game of chess and in particular, chess puzzles. The hitchhiker told the driver that he had recently discovered the most gripping chess puzzle that he had ever found; in fact, the best in the world. As by now the lights of Carlisle were in view, the hitchhiker told the driver where he lived and invited him to call, if he was ever nearby, and he would give him the puzzle that he kept behind the wooden carriage clock on his mantle piece.

On the outskirts of Carlisle, the driver stopped the car and his passenger climbed out, strolling towards the housing estate before simply vanishing into the mist. A few days later, and fancying a chess puzzle to occupy him through his Christmas break, the commercial traveller decided to drive to the address he'd been given. He found the house, walked up to the door and knocked, expecting it to be opened by the hitchhiker.

However, the door was opened by a woman in a black cardigan, with a pale face and tear-stained red eyes. The traveller told her that he had recently given her husband a lift home from Shap. At this the woman burst into tears, sobbing uncontrollably. Collecting herself, she invited the traveller in for a cup of tea; over the cup of tea she informed him that her husband had died in a car accident exactly one year ago on 'that bad bend' on the A6 by the churchyard in Shap. This caused another bout of helpless sobbing. Shaking with emotion himself, the traveller glanced across to the mantle piece. There, behind the carriage clock, he could see the corner of a folded piece of paper. Excusing himself, he leant across and took the piece of paper. Reading the contents, he discovered that it was indeed the finest chess puzzle he had ever seen. More importantly, it left him with an even bigger puzzle: 'The Puzzle of Mortality'.

The Ghost Ship

Whenever seamen meet and yarn there are stories of ghost ships, the Marie Celeste *being the best known of them all. As Cumbria has many ancient and busy harbours along its 150 miles of coastline, it would be strange if we didn't have a ghost ship. The following is a fairly dark Christmas story.*

In the days when the Cumbrian ports were still an integral part of the slave trade, the poor souls, once landed, were marched across the county. They often overnighted in great houses such as Storrs Hall, on the eastern shore of Windermere, en route for the slave markets of Manchester.

One Christmas Eve, the *Betsy Jane* was sailing down the Solway Coast. The poor captive souls onboard, weakened by their long voyage, could hear the sounds of Christmas bells ringing out from the churches of the nearby coastal villages and towns.

> Sweet bells, sweet bells, sweet chiming Christmas bells,
> Sweet bells, sweet bells, sweet chiming Christmas bells,
> They cheer us on our heavenly way, sweet chiming bells.

The captain and crew only had thoughts of the wealth that was awaiting them when their cargo was discharged. In fact, they were so distracted by their thoughts of gold that the ship crashed into the treacherous Giltstone Rock. The ship smashed and sank with the loss of captain, crew and cargo, even as the bells were ringing on land.

To this day, as Christmas church bells ring out in Maryport, Allonby and Silloth, the ghost of the skipper tries once again to dock his vessel, a task that always proves impossible – so the ghost ship *Betsy Jane* sails on, never to reach port. She is occasionally sighted by keen-eyed local folk making their way home from their carol service to celebrate a family Christmas.

The Mistletoe Bough

*The Gothic narrative that follows in the form of a popular song has
a varied and interesting history. Many ancient British houses display
wooden chests that the owners claim to be the cause of the demise of an
unfortunate bride at a Christmas wedding.*

*In fact it was the English writer Samuel Rogers who, on a visit to Italy
in the nineteenth century, came across a large oak chest in a Medina
mansion. Hung above the chest was the painting of a young woman who
purportedly perished in the chest when she became accidentally trapped
during a game of hide and seek with her new husband. Turning the
legend into a poem, 'Ginevra' Rogers brought it home to England.*

*In time, Bayly and Bishop turned the legend into a parlour song popu-
larly sung at Christmas in Victorian and Edwardian times. This song
survived into the twentieth century, indeed until the present day. It is still
sung to good effect by my friend, the Yorkshire dry stone waller, Will Noble.*

The mistletoe hung in the castle hall,
the holly branch shone on the old oak wall;
and the Baron's retainers were blithe and gay,
And keeping their Christmas holiday.
The Baron beheld with a father's pride,
His beautiful child, young Lovell's bride;
while she, with her bright eyes seemed to be,
The star of the goodly company.
Oh the mistletoe bough.

'I'm weary of dancing now' she cried,
'Here tarry a moment, I'll hide – I'll hide;
And Lovell, be sure thou'rt the first to trace
The clue to my secret lurking place,'
Away she ran, and her friends began,
Each tower to search, and each nook to scan,
And young Lovell cried, 'O where dost thou hide!
I'm alone without thee, my own dear bride.'
Oh the mistletoe bough

They sought her that night, and they sought her next day,
And they sought her in vain while a week passed away,
In the highest ... the lowest ... the loneliest spot,
Young Lovell sought wildly, but found her not.
And years flew by, and their grief at last,
Was told as a sorrowful tale long past;
And when Lovell appear'd, the children cried,
'See the old man weeps for his fairy bride.'
Oh the mistletoe bough.

At length an old chest that had long lain hid,
Was found in the castle ... they raised the lid ...
And a skeleton form lay mouldering there,
In the bridal wreath of that lady fair,
Oh sad was her fate! ... In sportive jest,
She hid from her lord in the old oak chest ...
It closed with a spring! ... And dreadful doom,
The bride lay clasp'd in her living tomb.
Oh the mistletoe bough.

Thomas Haynes Bayly and Sir Henry Bishop

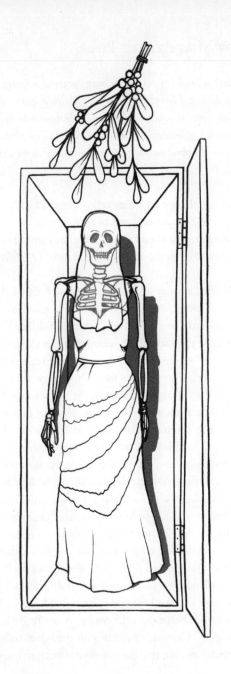

The Cow that Ate the Piper

The tale that follows has existed for many years as a rarely sung tradi-tional Irish ballad. I heard Yorkshireman Malcolm Storey deliver it at Whitby Folk Festival and heard a similar version told by Welshman Daniel Morden at one of our many meetings. The perfect chilling winter story – the ghost only makes an appearance in the dying seconds of the tale.

Many years ago there were pipers called 'Street Pipers', who would travel the land composing and playing a tune or 'planxty' in exchange for a meal or a bed for the night. The name of the host was then incorporated into the tune title for all time, i.e. 'Planxty Irvine'.

There was once a piper who had walked so far that the tops of his boots had come away from the bottoms, so when he walked down the road they went Schloop! Schloop! Schloop! This didn't really matter in the warmth of summer but in the winter, when there was snow on the ground, the snow and ice would get into his boots and lodge between his toes. This sort of did matter! One day our piper was traipsing through the snow towards a village where he reckoned on a good welcome. His foot bumped against a solid object in the snow. Bending down, he brushed away the snow to reveal … a head. It was the head of some poor bearded man who had fallen and frozen to death in the snow. Continuing to brush away the snow, he discovered the head was attached to a neck and the neck to a body. Carrying on with his brush-ing, he found two stiff legs. At the bottom of these two legs were feet wearing two fine brown tacketty boots. At a glance the piper realised the boots on the corpse were not only better than his own battered ones, but guessed them to be about his size. Part of him knew that nothing good ever came from stealing from a dead man. Our piper, however, was pragmatic and realised that he had more use for the brown boots than the corpse. Accordingly he thought 'finder's keepers'. Our hero tried to pull the boots from the feet. It was so cold, however, that the boots had frozen to the socks and the socks had frozen to the corpse. Luckily the bagpipes are a very temperamental instrument, so all pipers carry with them a tiny tool bag. The piper squatted down on his 'honkers' and rested the right leg of the dead man across his knees. From his tool bag he took out a tiny hammer and chisel. Tap, tap, tap, he chipped a tiny groove around the leg of the corpse just above the sock. There was no blood, for it was so cold that the blood had frozen solid in the veins of the body. Then our hero took a small hacksaw from his bag, placed the blade in the groove and sawed the foot clean off. Where he had cut through the shin, it was all pink like an uncooked burger. The task was half done. Dropping the stump of the right leg, he rested the left leg across his knees and repeated the operation. Tap, tap, tap, followed by a graunching sawing. Tying the bootlaces together and calmly replacing his tools in the pipe bag, he hung the severed feet around his neck like a gory necklace. The piper thought if he could find somewhere to thaw out his gruesome swag, he could have his boots.

Some way down the road, the piper spotted the friendly lights of a farmhouse gleaming up a lane. Thinking it might be a likely spot for a bite of scran and a shelter for the night, the piper strode up to the front of the house and peeped through the window. A table in the middle of the room was groaning with food and drink – a crusty cottage loaf, a truckle of cheese, a flagon of cider and a bottle of the finest malt whiskey were all there to tempt the hungry and thirsty piper. With fingers crossed, the piper rang the doorbell by tugging the brass chain. After some time the traveller could hear a heavy footfall approaching the front door. A brusque and unfriendly farmer spotted the travel-worn piper, who was incidentally using his folded arms to conceal his gory secret. He told the stranger in no uncertain terms to make himself scarce. The piper pleaded for sanctuary for the night, offering the reluctant host a pipe tune in the morning. The farmer, who had been enjoying a peaceful night at home, melted a little at the prospect of his own planxty and told the stranger he could sleep in the byre with Daisy the cow. The piper realised that he had slept in far worse places than that, for you do if you are an itinerant musician, and accepted the offer.

The byre had a big hole in the thatched roof, allowing the wind and the sleet to sweep in. Opening the half-door, the piper was introduced to Daisy the cow for the first time. Steam was coming out of her mouth and a faint stream of condensation was emitting from her nostrils. The piper thought that if he could somehow snuggle up against her rough hide for the night, she would keep him passably warm till the morning. He also thought to devise a way to melt the severed feet and avail himself of his new pair of boots. Accordingly, he laid the feet and the boots tied together on the pile of hay in the corner and persuaded Daisy to lie on top of them. He snuggled up to her, exhausted after the long journey along the road, and soon fell asleep. With the first light of day the piper woke up and slid his hand under the cow's belly. The feet still felt cold but there was something sticky and wet on his fingers. At a glance he realised it was blood, and yes, the feet had partially melted. He took hold of the soggy right ankle and pulled the foot from the boot, tossing it down on the straw. He took hold of the left ankle and pulling the dead man's foot from the boot, tossed it into the straw. He kicked off his old boots and looked at them against the pink, flaccid, severed feet. Trying on his newly acquired boots, he was delighted to discover they were a perfect fit. Job done! Daisy the cow had by now stood up and was gently chewing the cud. Looking up at Daisy and then down at his feet and the old boots, our hero had a wicked idea for a practical joke. He stood the severed feet in his old boots and placed them directly below the masticating mouth of Daisy the cow. Our hero then hid behind the straw bales and waited. Some time later, the farmer's wife came across the yard with a pint mug of tea for her guest and a three-legged stool and bucket to milk the cow. She opened the byre door and gazed at Daisy chewing slowly. She looked down at the feet and recognised the old boots. She looked up at the cow and down at the feet. She put two and two together and, making five, screamed hysterically that the cow had eaten the piper. Hearing the cries, the farmer crossed the yard. He too looked up at the cow and down at the boots.

He agreed with his wife that the cow had indeed eaten the piper and feared that if the police heard of this they would arrest the cow and there would be no more milk, no more butter and no more cheese. The piper, by now choking with guffaws of laughter, had slipped out of the back door of the byre and was legging it up the lane. Not unreasonably, the farmer and his wife decided that the only thing to do was to give the feet a decent burial and keep quiet about the whole affair. To accomplish this, he got the gruesome remains on a shovel and carried them to the middle of the fifteen-acre field. There he dug the smallest grave there has ever been (about two foot!) and buried the evidence before returning to the warmth of his fire and his 'still shaking' wife. At the end of the lane the piper, calming down a little, realised he hadn't played his host a tune in exchange for his night's accommodation. This was bad form. To put matters right he started to tune up his pipes and walked resolutely across the fifteen-acre field. In the farm the farmer and his wife heard the skirl of the pipes and rushed to the window. Looking out they saw the piper still playing, stepping over the very spot where the farmer had just buried the feet. Believing it to be the ghost of the piper, the luckless pair ran screaming out of the house and up the road to safety. The piper, meanwhile, saw the fleeing pair disappearing into the distance and realised he could enter the house and avail himself of the comestibles therein. He was just stood warming his backside at the fire, with a mug of mulled cider, when there was a knock at the front door.

Opening the door, the piper discovered an old man shivering, with snow in his hair, snow in his jacket and snow in his beard. The piper invited the stranger to come in close to the fire to warm his feet. The frozen old man retorted that he would … if he had any!

THE TURNING OF THE YEAR

'The Snow Falls, and the Wind Calls,
and the Year Turns Round Again'

John Tams

The Dragon of Winter

Some years ago I was invited to perform in the small seaside town of Silloth for their Kite Festival. There was no wind blowing that day but that is another story. Especially for that day, I crafted and performed the story that follows. The bones of the tale come from an old traditional legend I absorbed somewhere on my travels. Storytellers are naturally acquisitive and the tale surfaces every year when spring threatens to arrive.

It was the iron winter. The Dragon of Winter had curled itself around Scafell Pike, with its icy scales and tail sliding down into Lakeland and towards the Furness Peninsula. The rivers Duddon and Greta were frozen solid; even part of the sea was frozen at Whitehaven and Maryport. Wastwater, the deepest lake in the country, was frozen so solid that the good people of Wasdale were able to safely skate on it from end to end. Ships couldn't sail into the port of Whitehaven with food from foreign parts. All the people who lived in West Cumbria fell on hard times.

They went to the pompous mayor and told him that he would have to do something about the situation. The mayor knew he would have to go and reason with the dragon and persuade him to fly elsewhere, so he put on his climbing boots and warm clothes. Slipping and sliding he climbed up Scafell Pike, until he was staring into the icy blue eyes of the Dragon of Winter.

He told the dragon that it was upsetting local folk as they were not getting enough food and they were freezing. Because of this, the dragon would have to go elsewhere.

The dragon told the mayor he was reluctant to leave as he loved Cumbria and the Cumbrian folk, and especially his lofty perch.

Regretfully the mayor insisted the dragon would have to go. The dragon asked where he might go. The mayor suggested the dragon could fly to the frozen north and make a home with the polar bears and the Inuit.

A tear came into the dragon's icy blue eye. This was his place. He didn't want to go. The mayor, although pompous, was kindly and realised a compromise was called for.

The mayor suggested the dragon could stay up on Scafell Pike for part of the year – the months that Cumbrians call winter. The time that the dragon spent in the frozen north would be the time that Cumbrians call summer. The time when the dragon was flying north would be called spring. The time that the dragon was flying back would be called autumn. That was agreed and the mayor returned down the mountain to the towns and villages, where he told his people that the problem had been solved. They were delighted and told him he had done well, for they knew he had been very brave to climb the mountain and face the dragon.

The following day the Dragon of Winter spread its white leathery wings, flew high into the sky and headed for the north. The day after that, the sun came out bright and strong. The fishermen could go out and fish from Whitehaven Harbour and ships from afar could again bring food into the ports of West Cumbria.

All the people had smiles on their faces and all was well.

When autumn came it started to get cold again, and again the Dragon of Winter returned to its favourite place and curled itself around the peak of Scafell Pike. All the people were cold, but consoled themselves with the thought that the dragon would soon fly away. But when it came time for winter to end, the dragon was still there. Again the people went to the mayor, and the mayor realised that the dragon had forgotten the agreement. Although the families enjoyed playing in the snow and wearing warm jumpers and hearing stories by the fireside, again many were freezing and starving. The fishermen and farmers were struggling to work and again food supplies were running short. The dragon, once more, was to blame.

A young lad, toughened and wiry from working on his father's farm, was urged by his mates to tell the crowd that he could sort it. The crowd doubted whether such a youngster could possibly succeed where the mayor had failed. The unlikely hero put on his warm red hunting jacket and headed up the fell side, cheered on by his 'marras'. As he approached the dragon a mighty wind blew, tearing the red coat from the lad's back and floating it towards the dragon's icy blue eyes. Terrified, the dragon spread its wings and flew off to the frozen north. The hero retrieved his coat, heading back to the town to tell everyone the story of what had happened and to join the celebrations for the start of spring.

Ever since that day, as spring is due to arrive, folk in West Cumbria use the wind to fly pieces of coloured fabric on strings high into the sky. Most people think they are just flying these kites for fun, but a few know they are flying them to frighten away the Dragon of Winter.

The New Year's Bell

This story was gifted to me by a woman who is captain of the bell ringers in South Tawton, Devon.

Two communities had been at war. They'd lost much of their land, many of their men, but worst of all, they'd lost hope.

A couple of months after the last battle, a battle-blinded survivor wandered into his enemy's village. To his amazement, folk came from their homes to help him. They fed him, cared for him and gave him sanctuary. He told his newfound friends that before the war he had been a bell maker. He was so touched by their kindness that he offered to thank them by making a new bell. Folks smiled pityingly – how could a blind man make a decent bell? He set to work replacing sight with memory and soon crafted a bell that looked good. He told the villagers he would hang the new bell in the village bell tower and ring it for the first time on New Year's Eve.

In December, they helped the blind man up the ladder with the bell and it was hung in the old stone tower.

On New Year's Eve the villagers all gathered near the tower with cotton wool in their ears, for how could a blind man make a decent bell? The blind man climbed the ladder, grasped the rope and confidently struck the clapper on the bell. The sound that rang out was the purest, most perfect sound that has ever come from a bell. The crowd cheered. The blind man, however, had been so close to the bell and the note was so perfect, that something deep in his brain was disturbed and his sight restored.

That is why every New Year's Eve throughout these islands, bells are rung. They're rung for peace, they're rung for joy, but most of all they're rung for hope.

The Apple Tree Man

When Somerset storyteller and folklorist Ruth Tongue was a child, she wandered into an orchard with a friend. Gazing at an ancient gnarled apple tree, the young girl told Ruth it was the 'Apple Tree Man'. This fed Ruth's imagination and, when I was taken to meet her in the 1970s, she told me the stories of 'Tibb's Cat' and the 'The Apple Tree Man', two stories that mentioned this venerable tree sprite. Over the years of my storytelling with folk theatre company Magic Lantern, these mutated into one tale. The dialect is kept in the following version as it is the poetry of the country people and that I grew up with on my grandfather's farm.

There was this hard-working chap, as was the eldest of a long family line, so when his dad died there weren't nothing left for ee, the youngest brother gets it all for ee would be fitter to work the farm. Even though in this case ee was a lazy spoilt hosebird, so all he do let the oldest have was his dad's 'old dunk' (that's a donkey), an ox that had gone to anatomy (that's a skeleton) and a tumbledown cottage with two or dree old apple trees where his dad had used to live to with his grandfer. The oldest brother ee didn't grumble as a lot of folks would, no he went cutting the grass along the lane, and he fed it to the dunk, and thic old dunk began to fatten himself up and walk smart. Then he rubbed the ox's side with herbs and said the words, magic words, and thic old ox began to perk himself up. They old apple trees began to flourish a marvel with the beasts being in the orchet. All this work didn't leave ee no time to find his rent: O yes, youngest brother had to have his rent, dap on the dot too, greedy young guzzle bag!

One day the youngest brother stormed into the orchet and muttered, 'Tomorrow t'will be Christmas Eve when beasts do talk, we all know there's a treasure buried hereabouts and I am all set to ask your dunk and your ox where tis hid too. Wake me up just afore midnight and I'll knock a whole sixpence off your rent,' and off goes greedy young hosebird.

Well, as he said, the following day was Christmas Eve and, come nightfall, who should come wandering into the orchet but the little cat from down Tibb's farm, not much more than a kitten she were, a dairymaid of a cat (that's a black cat that's dipped her nose in a saucer of cream), and you know what they say about curiosity and the cat! So here er was in the orchet, owl-light on Christmas Eve, when out popped the Apple Tree Man. The Apple Tree Man shouted, 'You get on home my dear, this be no place for you, there's folks coming tonight to fire guns, drew my branches and pour cider drew my roots … you git on home and don't ee come back yer again until St Tibb's Eve.'

The little kitten shot off with her tail stiff with fright, properly scared she the Apple Tree Man did, and er never went back in the orchard again cos er didn't know when St Tibb's Eve wer! You and I know it's the night before St Tibb's Day!

Whilst all this wer gain on, the older brother, he put a sprig of holly up in the shippon (that's the cow shed) and gave his dunk and his ox a bit extra food to last them through Christmas Day cos he weren't gain to work that day. Then he took his last jug of cider and mulled it in front of the ashen faggot, then out to the orchet to give it to the apple tree. His was just pouring the cider down drew the roots when out popped the Apple Tree Man. The Apple Tree Man boomed, 'You look under this gurt didocky root of mine and you'll find something to do ee a bit of good.' So he looked under the root and he found a chest of the finest gold. 'Tis yourn and no-one else's,' said the Apple Tree Man, 'you put it away safe and bide quiet about im. Now you can call your dear brother and tell him tis midnight.'

Well the youngest brother came rushing out into the orchet in a terrible hurry push, and sure enough the dunk was talking to the ox, 'You do mind thic gurt greedy fule that's listening to we so unmannerly – ee do want we should tell ee where the treasures hid too.'

'And that's were ee aint gonna get it,' said the ox. 'Somebody have took ee already.' And do you know that was the last words they two beasts ever spoke. However, even to this day in the West Country we still:

Wassail the trees that they may bear
Many an apple and many a pear,
For the more or less fruit they will bring,
As we do give them wassailing.

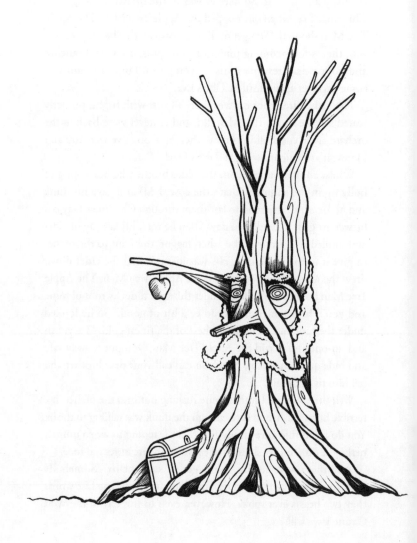

Wassailing

Wassail or Wes Hale in old English simply means 'Be whole or good health' as in hale and hearty! So the nationwide tradition of carolling wassail songs to friends and neighbours in the community is simply well wishing over the Christmas/New Year period. However, in some areas – notably those famous for apple orchards – the custom was to wassail not the local inhabitants but the apple trees. The logic is plain: healthy apple trees mean more apples, and more apples mean more cider. In addition to heartily toasting and singing to the trees, buttered toast is placed in the twigs to feed the robins who bring good luck. In an act of sympathetic magic, some hot spicy cider is poured into the roots, although much more is consumed by the singers (birds can't sing without seed!), as the cup is circulated.

> *Cinnamon, ginger, nutmeg and cloves*
> *and brandy gave me my jolly red nose*

Finally, to herald the toast, shotguns are fired through the branches of the trees – after shooing the robins away. Perhaps these old customs remind us of powers we once had but may be in danger of losing. Perhaps the powers of communities coming together to celebrate made them work harder and make their own luck for a better harvest.

In Carhampton and most other West Country communities where the custom is still practised, it takes place on old Twelfth Night, 17 January. However, the story that follows is set at Christmas. It is one of the riches that were gifted to me by the remarkable Ruth Tongue on one of my several visits to her cottage in Crowcombe, Somerset to find stories in the 1970s.

Somerset Wassail

Wassail and wassail all over the town
The cup it is white and the ale it is brown
The cup it is made of the good ashen tree
And so is the malt of the best barley

Chorus: For it's your wassail and it's our wassail
And it's joy to be to you and a jolly wassail

Oh master and missus, are you all within?
Pray open the door and let us come in
O master and missus a-sitting by the fire
Pray think on us poor travellers, a travelling in the mire

Oh where is the maid with the silver-headed pin
To open the door and let us come in
Oh master and missus, it is our desire
A good loaf and cheese and a toast by the fire

There was an old man and he had an old cow
And how for to keep her he didn't know how
He buile up a barn for to keep his cow warm
And a drop or two of cider will do us no harm

The girt dog of Langport he burnt his long tail
And this is the night we go singing wassail
O master and missus now we must be gone
God bless all in this house until we do come again

Toast To The Apple Tree

Old apple tree we wassail thee
And hoping thou wilt bear
Hats full, caps full
Three bushel bags full
And little heaps under the stair
Hip Hip Hooray

Since the days of my folk theatre company, Magic Lantern, I have followed the tradition of the story and this toast by passing around a wassail cup of hot, spicy cider.

TAFFY'S WASSAIL RECIPE

Wassail your trees that they may bear
Many an apple and many a pear.
For the more or less fruit they will bring
As you do give them wassailing.

Ingredients:

1 pint of dry cider (preferably Somerset farmhouse)
Slice of root ginger (size of postage stamp)
2" of cinnamon stick
2 tbs soft dark brown sugar
6 cloves
Fresh grated nutmeg to taste

Method:

Prostrate yourself towards Somerset! Combine
ingredients in a saucepan over a medium heat.
Stir with a wooden spoon.

If serving in a punchbowl then
roasted apples may be floated
on the mixture.

So here's to thee old apple tree,

That thou mayst blow

And thou mayst bow

And that thou mayst have apples a-mo'.

Hats full, caps full, three bushel bags full

.... and little heaps under the stairs.

Was'ail!

John Crane '91

Fairy Gold

This story is a valued link to my storytelling friends who are members of Scotland's Travelling People.

It was the turning of the year when an itinerant Scottish piper was tramping across the Perthshire hills. He was a welcome addition at any festivities as he was adept at playing the 'Goose'. This simplest of all Scots bagpipes comprises a mouthpiece, a bag and a chanter (the chanter is the pipe with finger holes from which tunes can be squeezed) while, in the interest of simplicity, the drone pipes are dispensed with. The whole contraption resembles a tartan version of the poultry after which it is named. Although he had worked hard, Hogmanay was approaching and he still needed more money to look after his wife and family. A day busking at Perth market would probably take care of this. The snow was deep on the ground but our hero was determined. He pulled on his tacketty boots and set out with his pipes under his arm. Trailing through the snow tired him, and halfway to Perth he needed a rest. Ahead he saw a mound of snow. Exhausted, he sat on the hillock and tuned his pipes. To his amazement, the hill started to move and cracked open. Our hero realised he had settled on top of a fairy fort, a hollow hill where the little people lived. A tiny man popped his head out of the crack in the hillock. Our hero stopped playing to stare at this wee man with a bright yellow suit, a pointy hat and two tiny wings. The fairy man commended our hero on his musical prowess, telling him that his king, the King of the Fairies, was famed for his Hogmanay parties. The snow was so deep that the king's party might be cancelled as the dance band were stuck in the snow some miles away. However, if our hero would play for the dancing, he would be paid a bag of fairy gold. The traveller realised that even if he busked at Perth market all day, he couldn't earn a bag of gold. How could he refuse such a generous offer? In short he couldn't so, grasping his pipes, he followed the little man through the crack into the fairy fort.

They entered a long hall and sitting on a big wooden throne was a very old man with a crown and a long white beard, the King of the Fairies. The king welcomed the piper, calling for a wooden stool to be placed in front of his throne. He repeated the promise to our hero of a bag of fairy gold in exchange for his music and called for everyone to take the floor for the first dance – 'The Gay Gordons'. The piper struck up with 'Scotland the Brave' on the 'Goose'.

Scotland the Brave

From every remote crevice of the fort, tiny people appeared and couples started birling (spinning) around the dance floor. As the music stopped there was applause, followed by a short encore of the same dance. Then it was supper time. Out of the kitchen poured the fairy cooks, each with a tray on their heads. Those trays contained fairy cakes and flower head cups containing mead. The piper had been warned by his mother and his grandmother never to accept presents from the fairies, lest they have him in their power. Our piper, however, was never a man to turn down a drink; and wasn't he thirsty? He quickly swilled down a cup of mead followed by a fairy cake and another couple of cups of the strong honey drink. Then it was time for 'Auld Lang Syne'.

Auld Lang Syne

The little people formed a circle linking crossed hands, just as we still do every New Year's Eve. Our piper ripped into a rousing jig at the end of a song before bowing to the King of the Fairies to tumultuous applause. The king put his hand under his cape, pulled out a leather pouch with the payment of fairy gold and told the piper he was free to leave. Bowing, the piper looked around the cave to see that it was completely sealed. He was trapped! He begged the king for help and the elderly monarch stamped his foot, pointing a hand towards the end wall of the cave. The wall cracked open. The piper peered outside, expecting to see deep snow and his own footprints leading into the fort. To his amazement he saw it was a bright spring day with no sign of snow. How long had he been playing for that party? He thought it had been a matter of hours but in fact it had been several weeks, for the fairies had kept him under their spell.

Blinking in the spring sunshine, our hero became angry that his time had been stolen. In a temper he grasped his bag of fairy gold, hurling it at a rock so hard it split open, scattering the pieces of gold in the bushes. Now those bushes were gorse and broom bushes. To this day, when spring arrives those bushes are covered with bright golden flowers. Well, I used to think they were flowers, but ever since hearing this story I realise they are not flowers at all, but pieces of 'Fairy Gold'.

To this day, Scotland's itinerant Travelling People winter in the towns and cities and only take to the road again when the 'yellow's on the broom', as my mentor Scots Traveller Duncan Williamson wrote in a song for his Scots Traveller friend Betsy Whyte (another of my mentors).

O come sit beside me Maggie love
I hate to see you gloom,
For I will take you on the road
When the yellow's on the broom.

Up Helly Aa

*In the 1980s I found out that Shetland boasts a January fire festival,
Up Helly Aa, which pays homage to its Viking past.*

*I decided to investigate, booking a flight to Lerwick and a B&B
with Mrs Jeannie Bain, aunt of the Shetland fiddle maestro Aly Bain.
When I asked about the festival, Mrs Bain put me right. She told me
that she could get me a ticket for a 'hall'. I discovered that this meant
I would have access to the all-night celebration dance after the fire,
where the Guiser squads would be called to perform their 'party pieces'.
The Guiser Jarl squad, however, the only ones in full Viking regalia,
would only have to turn up to be the stars of the celebration.*

*Mrs Bain told me to make my way to the town square to the unveil-
ing of the Joke Board. This was a hand-painted placard with scurrilous
satirical jests about local characters. This part of the festivities was
organised by the jokes committee. I immediately warmed to any community celebration that included a jokes committee. I then made my
way to the boat shed, where the beautiful Viking longboat was under
construction. I marvelled that such craftsmanship was being invested
in something that was to be paraded through the town before being
ceremoniously consigned to flames.*

*I observed on the bow of the boat that there was a pole with a carved
hand on the end. On enquiring about the significance of this, an old
man told me the story that follows.*

The Hand of Olaf

A thousand years ago, when the Viking invaders sailed west from Scandinavia, their first landfall was the Shetland Isles. The master of each craft was a 'jarl', a word that we have kept in use as 'earl'. Each jarl had a squad of men bent over the oars, rowing under threat of a whipping. One jarl, Olaf, was particularly fierce. On sighting land, the jarls agreed that whoever could set hand on the shore first could claim ownership of that land. Thus it would not be unusual for two longboats, in the final miles of their voyage, to be racing for a beach.

One day Olaf and his crew were heading towards the remote Shetland isle of Foula when he noticed, alongside, another longboat with the same goal. Olaf whipped his crew to row harder, realising as he did so that he might lose this particular race. As the boats approached the shore he pulled the knife from his belt with his right hand, using it to hack off his own left hand. The severed hand landed on the decking with a terrible splat. The oarsman nearest to Olaf quickly pulled out his leather bootlace and used it to staunch the bleeding from the stump. The jarl then bent down, picked up the severed hand with his good hand and flung it on to the beach, claiming ownership of the island as his hand had touched it first. Despite the moans and curses from the other longboat, Olaf's men cheered in triumph.

A triumph which is remembered each January, in all its gruesome glory, as the people of Shetland celebrate this wintery festival.

THE TWELVE MONTHS

The story that follows is a magical tale, perfect for January and wide-spread throughout Europe. It came to me from my friend, American teller of tales, Dan Keding. Although from Chicago, many of Dan's favourite tales hail from his Slavic roots, being given to him by his 'Nona', or grandmother, when he was a child. Dan and I trade stories at every available opportunity, each of us quickly adapting the story to make it our own. The motifs from the story that follows can be seen every January in Britain as we settle back to enjoy that very British tradition of pantomime with 'old friends' such as Cinderella and Snow White.

A generous-spirited young girl lived in a cottage on the edge of a forest with her mean-spirited stepmother and her selfish stepsister.

One New Year's Day the stepmother told the kind young girl that her stepsister's birthday was approaching and, giving her a basket, ordered her to go through the snow into the dark forest to pick snowdrops for her. The girl told the mother that it was far too early in the year for flowers, even snowdrops. However, the grumpy woman insisted and, as the stepsister sniggered behind her hand, the girl bravely grabbed the basket and a blanket and set off through the snow. The snow deepened and the sky darkened, but as she got closer to the forest, a light appeared through the trees ahead of her. As she walked towards the mysterious light, her nostrils twitched and she smelt woodsmoke. She reached a clearing in the forest where, to her amazement, she came upon twelve stone seats set around a fire.

Sitting on the seats were twelve men dressed in fine clothes of gold, silver, green and yellow: three of the strange men on the seats were very old, three were middle-aged, three were youths, and closest to the fire sat three young boys. In the largest seat at the back was an old man with long white hair, a long white beard and long bushy white eyebrows clutching a long ice-covered staff. The old man asked who the girl was and what she wanted. The girl told him that she had been sent by her stepmother to pick snowdrops and could he please help. The old man told her that it was too early in the year to pick flowers, as spring couldn't come before winter was over. Crying, the girl told him that if she failed in her task she would be beaten. Again she politely pleaded for help. The old man told her that he shouldn't help as he still had thirty and one days to rule. However, as she had been so gentle and polite, he would make an exception. He handed his staff to February, the old man next to him. February struck the staff on the ground, the ice fell from it and green buds began to sprout. The snow stopped falling and the snow on the ground melted to reveal snowdrops peeping out of the softening brown soil. The girl thanked them and rushed around collecting the blooms until her basket was full. February handed the staff back to January, who advised the girl to head home with the basket as quickly as she could.

As the girl hurried towards her cottage, ice again appeared on the staff and, as January struck the ground, the skies darkened again and the snow deepened.

Pushing open the cottage door, to the amazement of her stepmother and her stepsister, the girl tipped the snowdrops out on the table. She told them all that had happened but, far from being grateful, the greedy sister pointed out that she could have wished for strawberries, apples and pears instead of snowdrops in midwinter – items which they could have taken to market and sold for a fortune. The stepmother commended her greedy daughter for this idea and immediately sent her off in to the snow, telling her to find the twelve mysterious men and return with the fruit.

The mean-spirited girl followed her sister's footprints, thinking that she could do anything that her sister could do. She arrived at the fire in the clearing where the men were sitting in their stone seats. January guessed who she was and asked why she had come. The girl demanded strawberries, apples and pears without so much as a 'by your leave'. Strawberries in winter, the old man declared, were not possible, as summer could never come before spring and autumn could never come before summer. He told her that, if she wanted summer in winter, then she should seek it and pointed his icy staff towards the forest, far from the fire. The greedy stepsister quickly set off in this direction, dreaming of the riches she would

have when such fruits were sold at the market. As she moved further and further from the warmth of the fire, however, the cold gathered around her and, before long, she fell headlong in to a snowdrift and was swallowed up by the snow.

Back at the cottage, the stepmother waited impatiently for the gifts of fruit in winter. The generous young girl prayed for the safe return of her stepsister, with or without the fruit. When there was no sign of the girl after several hours, the stepmother could wait no more. She set out to search for her. Before long, lost, shouting and cursing, she found herself deep in the snow and, like her daughter, she too was swallowed up in the storm. Neither of them were ever seen again.

Back at the cottage, the kind, polite and hard-working girl waited for their return. But as winter turned to spring, they never did. She tended the cottage garden, which seemed to be beautiful with flowers and heavy with fruit whatever the season. Folk commented that her garden seemed to be visited by all twelve months at once. Perhaps it was.

EPILOGUE

JANUARY MAN

Whilst still a young man, my friend, songwriter Dave Goulder (who now lives in the Highlands of Scotland), wrote the perfect almanac song that follows. One of the finest songs I know, it perfectly follows the tale of 'The Twelve Months'.

> Oh the January man he walks abroad
> In woollen coat and boots of leather
> The February man still wipes the snow
> From off his hair and blows his hands
> The man of March he sees the Spring and
> Wonders what the year will bring
> And hopes for better weather.
>
> Through April rain the man goes down
> To watch the birds come in to share the summer
> The man of May stands very still
> Watching the children dance away the day
> In June the man inside the man is young
> And wants to lend a hand
> And grins at each newcomer.

And in July the man in cotton shirt
He sits and thinks on being idle
The August man in thousands takes the road
To watch the sea and find the sun
September man is standing near
To saddle-up and lead the year
And Autumn is his bride.

The man of new October takes the reins
And early frost is on his shoulder
The poor November man sees fire and wind
And mist and rain and Winter air
December man looks through the snow
To let eleven brothers know
They're all a little older.

And the January man comes round again
In woollen coat and boots of leather
To take another turn and walk along
The icy road he knows so well
The January man is here for
Starting each and every year
Along the way forever.

Dave Goulder

BIBLIOGRAPHY

As anyone who knows my work from previous publications or live performances will realise, most of my sources are oral and credited as such in the introductions to the stories. However, I regularly delve into my trusty archive of favourite books for both inspiration and material to add to my repertoire.

Cater, Colin and Karen, *Wassailing* (2013)
Davis, David, *A Single Star* (1973)
Keding, Dan, *Stories of Hope and Spirit* (2004)
Struthers, Jane, *Red Sky at Night* (2009)
Thomas, Taffy, *Cumbrian Folk Tales* (2012)
Tongue, Ruth, *Forgotten Folk Tales of the English Counties* (1970)
Walter, Elizabeth, *Seasons Greetings* (1980)

ABOUT THE AUTHOR

Taffy Thomas has been living in Grasmere for well over thirty years. He was the founder of legendary 1970s folk theatre company Magic Lantern, who used shadow puppets and storytelling to illustrate folk tales. After surviving a major stroke in 1985, he used oral storytelling as speech therapy, which led him to find a new career working as a storyteller. He set up the Storyteller's Garden and the Northern Centre for Storytelling at Church Stile in Grasmere, Cumbria. He was asked to become patron of the Society for Storytelling and was awarded an MBE for Services to Storytelling and Charity in the Millennium honours list. In January 2010 he was appointed as the first UK Storyteller Laureate at the British Library. He was awarded the Gold Badge, the highest honour of the English Folk Dance and Song Society that same year. At the 2013 British Awards for Storytelling Excellence (BASE), Taffy received the award for Outstanding Male Storyteller and also received the award for Outstanding Storytelling Performance for his piece 'Ancestral Voices'.

STORYTELLER

TAFFY
THOMAS
M.B.E
LAUREATE

PUT HIS PAWS

A DRAGON

A MAN WHO HAD

In Conclusion

It is my hope that this seasonal collection of folk tales has added to my previous publications in revealing the richness and variety of a living oral tradition. I accept that these stories may be better heard than read. Then why bother writing them down at all? Firstly, as I reach my 'third age', I am keen that my repertoire will outlive me. It probably will in the hands of my own three children and grand-child, plus all the people I have mentored and helped in their own steps down the storytelling road. Another motivation to commit my stories to print was my upbringing with my profoundly deaf cousin John Sprake. I think the deaf community should not be excluded from the pleasure of a wealth of folk tales, an aural tradition.

It is also my hope that my readers' pleasure will promote a more positive view of what is usually thought of as the most moribund and bleak of seasons. If we can only reacquaint ourselves with nature, this season can add variety to our lives; quite literally frost and fire.

Whilst holding this ideal, I am of course aware that I completed this manuscript amidst the most extreme winter spell of weather in living memory: wild, exciting, but not all good. Indeed my much-loved apprentice storyteller, Harry Swordy, at the age of twenty-seven, was swept from a Cornish beach to his death by a freak Atlantic wave in the early hours of New Year's Day in 2014. Harry treasured storytelling and, as a great listener, refused to sepa-rate it from nature, writing in his notebook:

'Nature is to be felt deep within our souls and listened to intently.'

If you feel close to these stories and a bit closer to nature, please pass them on as they only live by being told from one friend to another.

Lest I have driven you crazy with the riddles in Part 3 of this book, here are the answers.

Pass the riddles on quickly but reveal the answers slowly, just as I have.

Puzzle A: The man was a skydiver and his parachute hadn't opened
Puzzle B: Romeo and Juliet were fish and Felix was a cat

Riddle 1: Christmas Pudding
Riddle 2: Christmas Pudding
Riddle 3: Robin
Riddle 4: Snowflake
Riddle 5: Fire
Riddle 6: Coal
Riddle 7: Holly

Three Mince Pies: The two mothers and two daughters were a grandmother, a mother and a granddaughter

Horseplay: The two words were 'swap horses' (it's a riddle about ownership)

If you are interested in riddles, you may like the following book by Taffy Thomas, *The Riddle in the Tale*, also published by The History Press.

A Midwinter Toast

May you have a full moon to light you,
A straight road to dance down,
And warm words on a cold night.

The author

Also from The History Press

∧NCIENT LEGENDS RETOLD

This series features some of the country's best-known folklore heroes. Each story is retold by master storytellers, who live and breathe these legends. From the forests of Sherwood to the Round Table, this series celebrates our rich heritage.

Also from The History Press

We are proud to present our historical crime fiction imprint, The Mystery Press, featuring a dynamic and growing list of titles written by diverse and respected authors, united by the distinctiveness and excellence of their writing. From a collection of thrilling tales by the CWA Short Story Dagger award-winning Murder Squad, to a Victorian lady detective determined to solve some sinister cases of murder in London, these books will appeal to serious crime fiction enthusiasts as well as those who simply fancy a rousing read.

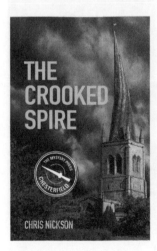

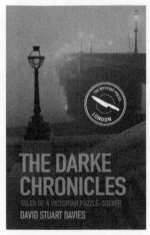

Find these titles and more at
www.thehistorypress.co.uk

Also from The History Press

More spooky Books